HANDBOOK OF THE MASS

George Fitzgerald, C.S.P.

Paulist Press

New York/Ramsey

The Publisher gratefully acknowledges use of the following: Excerpts from the English translation of *Lectionary for the Mass* © 1969, International Committee on English in the Liturgy, Inc. (ICEL); excerpts from the English translation of *Rite of Anointing and Pastoral Care of the Sick* © 1973, ICEL; excerpts from the English translation of the *Roman Missal* © 1973, ICEL. All rights reserved.

Library of Congress
Catalog Card Number: 82-81187

ISBN: 0-8091-2401-7

Published by Paulist Press
545 Island Road, Ramsey, N.J. 07446

Printed and bound in the
United States of America

To my parents

CONTENTS

PREFACE

Every once in a while, either at a home Mass or on a Sunday, I give a running commentary on the history, theology and development of the Mass. Almost always, several people express their appreciation and say: "I've never heard that before," or "I've always wondered what those words meant." Catholics from the cradle upward will say that they never have had an instruction on the Mass either in school or in religious ed courses.

"Going to Mass" is a given for most Catholics. It's their badge of identity with the Church. For many it's the most frequent way of staying in touch with God through Scripture and the Eucharist. Yet many know very little about the Mass.

At our parish at the University of California, Berkeley, the staff gave a four-week catechesis on the Mass based on some of this book's material. We divided the liturgy into its four main parts. The response was overwhelmingly favorable from students, professors, and families. The instruction brought a sense of unity and shared purpose. Participation in the liturgy increased. There was a sense in which a deeper knowledge of the Mass bridged the members of this highly diversified congregation. People asked for copies of the catechesis which we published weekly in order to send it to friends or for use in the family.

My thanks to Fr. Chris Witt, C.S.P., a Paulist at Ohio State University, for critiquing and strengthening parts of the manuscript. I am grateful to Ms. Gloria Ortíz for the design and art work in the book. I am also grateful to Fr. Larry Boadt, C.S.P., an editor at Paulist Press, who shepherded its pages to the printers after I left Paulist Press for a new assignment in 1980. I can only hope that this little work will, for some at least, be a first step toward a fuller and richer appreciation of the Mass.

INTRODUCTION

The History of the Mass

The Eucharist is the mystery of Jesus' presence with and for his community, the Church. It is the "mystery of faith" which the Church down through the ages has continuously unfolded. Over the centuries, the Eucharist has been called the Mass, the Breaking of the Bread, the *Synaxis,* the Lord's Supper, the *Dominicum Convivium,* the Holy Sacrifice, the Liturgy, the Sacred Mysteries, and Holy Communion. All of these designations have a special meaning and capture a dimension of this life-giving mystery which is the heart of Christian life.

Our understanding and appreciation of the Eucharist can be deepened by an understanding of the Church's constant search, from apostolic times to the present, for the full meaning of this great mystery. In this small volume we offer a brief overview of the history, theology and ritual of the Mass. Our aim is to provide the readers with an aid to deepen their appreciation of the Eucharist and to enrich their participation in the eucharistic celebration.

The New Testament

During the first few centuries the Church primarily spoke of the Eucharist as "the breaking of the bread" (Acts 2:42–46). Celebrated in private homes (Acts 2:46; 20:8; 1 Corinthians 16:19), the eucharistic service included instruction, homilies, prayers and the breaking of the bread (Acts 14:22; 15:32; 20:7, 11). The focus of the earliest celebrations was in the "remembering" that, on the night before he died, Jesus, according to the Jewish custom, shared bread and wine with his apostles and identified himself (his life, his body and his blood) with the bread and wine (1 Corinthians 11:23–25; Luke 22:19–20; Mark 14:22–24; Matthew 26:26–28).

The specifics of these earliest celebrations are not detailed. In some cases the earliest disciples continued to celebrate the Eucharist in the context of a larger meal, called an "agape" (1 Corinthians 11:20–22, 33–34). Abuses caused the discontinuance of this practice. The early celebrations also included prayers (Acts 2:42) spoken principally by "elders" who presided over the gatherings (Acts 6:4–6; 13:3), or by others known as "prophets" (Acts 13:3; 1 Corinthians 12:28).The eucharistic gatherings were often held in the early morning hours, and eventually on Sunday, linking the celebration to the Lord's resurrection ("early in the morning of the first day," John 20:1).

More specific details of the development of the Mass begin to appear at the end of the first century. As the Christian community began to grow, and the apostles and immediate disciples of the Lord began to die, the need for a more formal structure for the celebration of the Eucharist arose so that the tradition passed on by the apostles might be preserved.

The History of the Mass After the New Testament

The specifics of the celebration of the Eucharist become more detailed from the end of the first century. An examination of three important documents will help us appreciate both the growth of the structure of the Mass in the first centuries after Jesus and the ritual of the liturgy as we celebrate it today.

The Didache: The Teaching of the Twelve Apostles

The *Didache,* probably written toward the end of the first or the beginning of the second century, provides us with a link between the Judaic ritual that characterized the early eucharistic celebrations and the specifically Christian ritual that would be developed. This early document preserves for us a set of prayers which have a eucharistic character. While the origin and purpose of the prayers is not conclusive, they reflect typical prayers of thanksgiving brought to the Christian community by Jewish converts. A prayerful reading of the following excerpts from the *Didache* can enrich our appreciation of our eucharistic tradition:

Now about the Eucharist: This is how to give thanks. First in connection with the cup:

We thank you, our Father, for the holy vine of David, your child, which you have revealed through Jesus, your child. To you be glory forever.

Then in connection with the broken bread:

We thank you, our Father, for life and knowledge which you have revealed through Jesus, your child. To you be glory forever.

As this bread was scattered over the hills and then was brought together and made one, so let your Church be brought together from the ends of the earth into your kingdom. For yours is the glory and the power through Jesus Christ forever. After you have finished your meal, say grace in this way:

We thank you, holy Father, for your sacred name which you have lodged in our hearts, and for knowledge and faith and immortality which you have revealed through Jesus, your child. To you be glory forever. Almighty Master, you have created everything for the sake of your name, and have given men food and drink to enjoy that they may thank you. But to us you have given spiritual food and drink and eternal life through Jesus, your child. Above all we thank you that you are mighty. To you be glory forever. Remember, Lord, your Church, to save it from all evil and make it perfect by your love. Make it holy, and gather it together from the four winds into your kingdom which you made ready for it. For yours is the power and the glory forever.

The Judaic heritage of these prayers (blessings) is evident. In them we see the roots of our contemporary Christian eucharistic ritual, and can discover a sense of our "tradition" and "belonging" to the earliest celebrations of the Mass.

The Apology of Saint Justin Martyr (c. 150 A.D.)

In the middle of the second century, Saint Justin, a layman, philosopher, convert and martyr, refuted pagan accusations against Christian practices. In one of these writings, *The First Apology,* an outline of the structure of the Mass is found. The structure described by Justin is familiar to us today:

1. Scripture readings (including the "memoirs of the apostles")
2. Homily or sermon
3. Common prayers
4. Kiss of peace
5. Offertory
6. Eucharistic prayer with congregational "Amen"
7. Distribution of Communion

A reading of chapter 67 of Justin's *First Apology* provides us with the opportunity to discover how early in our tradition the Mass ritual we celebrate today received its basic structure:

"And on that day which is called after the sun, all who are in the towns and in the country gather together for a communal celebration. And then the memoirs of the apostles or the writings of the prophets are read, as long as time permits. After the reader has finished his task, the one presiding gives an address, urgently admonishing his hearers to practice these beautiful teachings in their lives. Then all stand up together and recite prayers. After the end of the prayers . . . the bread and wine mixed with water are brought, and the president offers up prayers and thanksgivings, as much as in him lies. The people chime in with an Amen. Then takes place the distribution, to all attending, of the things over which the thanksgiving has been spoken, and the deacons bring a portion to the absent (he had previously remarked, '. . . this food itself is known among us as the Eucharist. No one may partake of it unless he is convinced of the truth of our teachings and is cleansed in the bath of baptism . . .'). Besides, those who are well-to-do give whatever they will. What is gathered is deposited with the one presiding, who therewith helps orphans and widows. . . ."

The Apostolic Tradition of Saint Hippolytus (c. 200 A.D.)

While the writings of Justin provide us with a picture of the overall structure of the Mass, the form or structure of the eucharistic prayers were still somewhat flexible and left up to the discretion of the person presiding: "The president offers up prayers and thanksgivings, as much as in him lies." It is only with the *Traditio Apostolica* of Hippolytus, a Roman presbyter and martyr, that we possess an historical document that contains an explicit form of a eucharistic prayer. Written and prayed in Greek this prayer is still used by the Ethiopian Church, and was adopted by Rome as the model for Eucharistic Prayer II of the present Roman ritual.

The Lord be with you. And with your spirit. Up with your hearts. We have lifted them up to the Lord. Let us give thanks to the Lord. It is the proper and right thing to do.

We give thanks to you, O God, through your beloved servant Jesus Christ whom in these last days you have sent us as Savior, Redeemer and Messenger of your will; who is your Word inseparable from you, through whom you made all things and in whom you were well pleased. You sent him from heaven into the womb of the Virgin where he was made flesh and revealed as your Son, born of the Holy Spirit and the Virgin. Fulfilling your will and gaining for you a holy people, he stretched out his hands in his passion to free from suffering those who believed in you.

And when he was betrayed to the passion which he desired in order to destroy death, break the chains of the devil, tread on hell, enlighten the good, set a limit and manifest his resurrection, taking bread and giving thanks to you, he said: "Take, eat, this is my body which is broken for you." Likewise the chalice, saying: "This is my blood which is shed for you. When you do this, you remember me."

We therefore, remembering his death and resurrection, offer you the bread and the chalice, giving you thanks for graciously allowing us to appear before you and to serve you.

And we beg you to send your Holy Spirit upon the offering of the holy Church. Gathering all into one, grant that all the holy people who partake (of it) may be filled with the Holy Spirit and be strengthened in the faith of truth, so that we may praise and glorify you through your servant Jesus Christ, through whom be glory and honor to you, Father and Son with the Holy Spirit, in your holy Church, now and forever. Amen.

Thus from the very first centuries the basic forms of the Order of the Mass as we know it today began to emerge. The centuries that were to follow would draw upon these basic traditions and embellish them with rituals in order to gather together the Christian community to give thanks and praise to the Father by remembering the life, death, and resurrection of Jesus in the sacramental sacrifice of the Mass.

Later Developments: Constantine to Trent

By 370 the Mass was still simple in form. Liturgies in the East and West, while sharing in a common tradition, exhibited a diversity of rituals or forms of celebration. The Sunday, and not the daily, celebration of Mass was customary. The faithful still preserved the ancient practice of taking home a portion of the consecrated breads which they carefully preserved both for personal use and for distribution to the sick, shut-ins, prisoners, and the monks who lived in isolation.

With the continuing growth and spread of Christianity, important changes occurred in the ritual of the Mass. The small and more intimate worshiping communities became increasingly larger and impersonal. Worshipers became passive attendants, and gradually distant even from the reception of Holy Communion. Why? The reasons were many and complex, but in general were reflective of the many cultural and theological influences upon the expanding Church. Conditions became so critical by the year 400 that the Council of Toledo had to impress Christians with the importance of regularly attending the eucharistic celebration by threatening with excommunication those who stayed away from worship for three or four consecutive Sundays.

The next half of the century saw the attempts to establish more defined liturgical forms. The Canon of the Mass (Eucharistic Prayer) became more stable, and its basic framework was formed during the fourth through the sixth centuries. During the eighth century the Franks, under the leadership of Charlemagne, attempted to provide an even broader uniformity of liturgical practice throughout Europe. Liturgical books were organized, and rituals and ceremonies became more elaborate.

What was happening, and what would continue to happen, was the experience of the impact of culture upon the liturgical forms of Western Christianity. What were some of the effects of this impact?

The Dark Ages had fallen over Europe. The barbarian invasions disrupted learning and culture, and the people became more and more separated from the roots of early Christianity. Wars, famines, and plagues inflicted hardship and suffering. There was much cruelty in daily living. God seemed remote, distant, apart from a world of toil and trouble. People grew to feel unworthy to be in the presence of so mysterious and unapproachable a God. Culture also had its impact on the attitude of Christians toward Christ. The divinity of Christ began to overshadow his humanity. This reinforced an attitude of mystery and unapproachableness.

Such thinking had its inevitable effects on the liturgical actions of the community. By the fourteenth century the Mass had become more the action of the priest than of the community. Altars, once close to and facing the people, became separated from the laity by rails. Only those designated to participate in the celebration were allowed in the set-off, or holy, place (sanctuary). Priests offered Mass quietly with their backs to the people who now attended rather than participated in Mass. As the laity became silent observers of the sacred action they began to ask monks to pray for their needs and personal wishes ("votive Mass")—a custom which began during the eighth century. In return for such prayers the laity made an offering (stipend) toward the support of the Church. Increasing attention was focused on the benefits and graces which the offering of the Mass would bring in return for this offering.

The awareness of the Mass as a memorial of the Last Supper meal eventually diminished. The emphasis of the celebration shifted from meal to sacrifice. The center of the celebration for the laity became their act of adoration during the elevation of the host after the words of consecration silently spoken by the priest. The importance of Holy Communion as food for life also logically faded. The shift from Communion to adoration was taking place. This was evidenced in many ways. The faithful were no longer permitted to bake and provide the altar breads. Instead, nuns and monks who were considered more worthy of the task provided small, white wafers as "hosts." The Mass ritual became more and more embellished with gestures that reminded the celebrant of the sacrifice of

Christ—for example, the triple blessing of the host by the priest reminded him of the times the Lord was mocked during his passion. Genuflections abounded, stressing the fact that the focus had indeed become one of adoration rather than Communion. So deep was the shift that bishops and Councils pleaded with the laity to receive Holy Communion at least once a year (Easter duty).

Such developments were not without the parallel growth of many abuses. Among other issues, the Reformers of the fifteenth and sixteenth centuries criticized the seemingly unchecked growth of these eucharistic abuses.

Later Developments: Trent to Present

The Council of Trent (1545–1563) responded to the sixteenth-century Reformers by clarifying the teaching of the Church and by correcting the abuses which had arisen. One result of these measures was the Roman Missal of 1570 which for almost four centuries fixed the rites of the Mass. Abuses had grown so rampant that such rigidity was necessary.

During the twentieth century the rigid uniformity imposed by Trent began to be lessened. "Mass books" (missals) written in the language of the people began to appear. These enabled the laity to follow the Mass as the priest silently spoke its prayers in Latin. Pope Pius X (1903–1914) encouraged frequent reception of Holy Communion for both adults and children (1905). The "dialogue Mass" later appeared in response to the laity's growing awareness of their need to be part of the sacred action.

Pope Pius XII (1939–1958) encouraged the continuance of this trend toward a liturgical celebration involving the whole community. His contributions include the Holy Week reforms of 1955, the urging of greater participation of the laity, and the relaxation of fasting regulations to encourage more frequent reception of Communion.

The Second Vatican Council (1962–1965) synthesized these new trends in the Constitution on the Sacred Liturgy (1963). This document paved the way for the numerous adaptations of liturgical rites so that the liturgy became, in practice as well as in theory, the action of the total community. Each member of the community was encouraged to participate fully and actively according to defined roles. Altars were turned around. The language of the people (vernacular) was restored. The rites of the Mass were simplified and a new Missal was published in 1970. The aim of all this work was careful restoration—a bringing into the present the total liturgical heritage of the Christian community: "Elements which suffered injury through accidents of history are to be restored to the norms of the Holy Fathers . . . as rites are simplified with due care to preserve their substance" (Paul VI).

The Presence of Christ in the Mass

The history of the development and celebration of the Mass capsulizes the Christian community's deep faith in the presence of Christ among his people. From the very beginning, faith in the presence of the risen Lord has been the central mystery and claim of Christianity. This presence has been, is, and always will be the Christian source of hope and strength.

Every action of each Christian and the Christian community should exemplify this presence. The Christian mission to the world is to give witness to all others to the presence of the living Christ. This witness is most explicitly proclaimed and celebrated in the central action of the Christian community, the Eucharist. The Church reminds us: "For in this sacrament Christ is present in a unique way, whole and entire, God and man, substantially and permanently. This presence of Christ under the species 'is called *real* not in an exclusive sense, as if other kinds of presence were not real, but *par excellence*' " (Eucharisticum Mysterium, n. 9).

In order to heighten the awareness of the Christian community to the pervasiveness of the presence of Christ, Vatican II reflects on the ways in which Christ is present in the eucharistic assembly:

1. *In the assembly of believers:* Each Christian is called to recognize the presence of Christ through grace in each of his brothers and sisters. It is a sacrament of love: "If anyone says, 'My love is fixed on God,' yet hates his brother, he is a liar" (1 John 4:20). "Where two or three are gathered in my name, there am I in their midst" (Matthew 18:20).
2. *In the minister who leads the community in worship:* He recalls the words of Christ and speaks

sacramentally to the community so that Christ may be present celebrating this Eucharist with his people. The minister is a brother among brothers and sisters, since he, too, eats with the Lord.

3. *In the word of Scripture:* When the word of God is proclaimed and sung in responses, Christ touches the hearts and minds of his people.

4. *In the whole action of the Eucharist:* Christ draws the members of his body into perfect self-giving to the Father, and he shares with them the glory of his death and resurrection.

5. *In our food and drink:* Just as Christ changed the direction of humankind by his death and resurrection, so too he changes bread and wine into the new manna and nourishment of humankind. He now lives in us and through us drawing all people and all things to himself.

Ritual in the Mass

The celebration of the Mass expresses the identity of the Christian community. It is "the supreme means by which the faithful come to express in their lives and to manifest to others the mystery of Christ and the real nature of the true Church" (Constitution on the Liturgy, n. 2). Central to this expression are the words and actions, or the rituals, of that celebration. For these are the symbols which put us in touch with the reality of this great mystery of faith.

Men and women are ritual makers. Since they first experienced the world in awe and wonder, humans symbolized the meaning of that experience. They traced pictures on cave walls to express their feelings and beliefs. Drawings and carvings, religious celebrations and fiestas, in every age and place, are expressions of the human struggle to concretize the inner meaning of life.

Christian rituals and symbols have developed over the centuries. These rituals and symbols are like a door. They are an invitation to pass beyond what we see and to touch something or Someone greater than ourselves. They break through the limits of human life in order to reveal the holy and the sacred.

We greet one another daily. We seek forgiveness to repair and heal human life. Without pardon our world would be intolerable. We share memories of persons, places and events—often over a meal. We eat to live; we bless food, we offer thanks for love, hope, gifts given and received. Music, festivity, and color are signs of the specialness of human gatherings.

We ritualize meetings, birthdays, anniversaries, and deaths. We share a meal to discuss a serious matter, to heal past hurts, or to make promises for the future. We toast, kiss, hug and shake hands. Our meals are marked by graciousness and good feelings. Our meals help us grow in all ways.

All of these elements of life are reflected in the Mass. They are there because that is the way we are. Our words, our actions give expression to who we are and for what we hope. They help express what is most human and most sacred in us. Catholics live by the simple, everyday belief that their words and symbols express their identity, and that the ritual of the Eucharist is the summary, the summit, of that expression:

The Eucharist both perfectly signifies and wonderfully effects that sharing in God's life and unity of God's people by which the Church exists. It is the summit of both the actions by which God sanctifies the world in Christ and the worship which men offer to Christ and which through him they offer to the Father in the Holy Spirit. Its celebration "is the supreme means by which the faithful come to express in their lives and to manifest to others the mystery of Christ and the true nature of the Church" (Eucharisticum Mysterium, n. 6).

Liturgical Year and Church Calendar

The eucharistic rituals of the Church take place within the context of the liturgical year or "Church calendar." Just as the seasons of the earth alert us to the changing beauty of creation and its cyclic message of life through death, the Church's liturgical seasons unfold the life-producing mysteries of the salvation that comes through life in Christ.

The "Church calendar" provides us with the opportunity of sharing humankind's hope for life—a life revealed in Christ, his birth, his public ministry, his death, his resurrection, the sending of the Spirit, and the foundation of the Church. The "Church calendar" also helps the Christian community to deepen its identity as a people, and to give thanks to God for its past, present and future. Sunday commemorates the Lord's day—the life-assuring resurrection of the Lord. Special holy days celebrate significant events in the life of Jesus, Mary, and the Church. Feast days recall the lives and faith of special Christians, saints, as sources of inspiration for contemporary followers of the Lord. All the seasons of the Church's liturgical year and the events of the Church's calendar are the Church's human way of helping its members enter the mystery of Christ. A review of the Church year will help us take advantage of the opportunity it offers.

Advent is a time of expectation, preparation, and waiting for the coming of the Messiah. The Church recalls the long and stormy history of the Jewish people, reflects on the words of the prophets, and introduces John the Baptist. The Church also looks forward to the time when the purpose of Christ's coming will be fulfilled. Purple vestments are worn as a symbol of expectation (a turning toward Christ who is the hope of all creation).

Christmas is a time of joyful acknowledgement of Christ as Savior, God coming to dwell with his people. The role of Mary is acknowledged (January 1), and the nations proclaim Christ as the light of the world (January 6, the Epiphany)—the manifestation of God's love to all peoples. White vestments denote joy as a sign that God has come among us in Jesus.

Lent is a season of entering into the death of Jesus and of surrendering ourselves completely to the Father. The Church calls the faithful to a new and more profound conversion culminating in a renewal of their baptismal commitment during the Easter celebration. In a special way Lent is the season of final preparation for those seeking to become members of the Church (catechumens) and who will be baptized at the Easter vigil. The traditional actions of praying, almsgiving, and fasting are intensified to deepen one's relationship to God, others, and self. There are forty days of Lent, beginning on Ash Wednesday and continuing until Holy Thursday. Violet vestments remind us of our need for penance and conversion.

Holy Week/Easter Triduum celebrates the last days of the Lord by bringing us with Christ through death to the experience of a new life. Passion (Palm) Sunday commemorates the Lord's triumphal entry into Jerusalem and the foreshadowing of his death. Holy Thursday commemorates the institution of the Eucharist and the Lord's command to serve as he has served. Good Friday remembers the sacrifice of the cross, the pouring out of Christ's life to seal the new covenant which Christians enter through the waters of baptism. The Easter Triduum culminates in the Easter Vigil service where the meaning of Christ's life, and especially his death, is proclaimed: "Christ has died! Christ is risen! Christ will come again!"

Easter Season is a continuous feast of fifty days called the "Great Sunday." The Church continues to rejoice in the new life made possible in Jesus. As this season draws to a dramatic close, the acceptance of Christ's work by his Father is celebrated by remembering Jesus' triumphant return to the Father (Ascension Thursday) and his sharing that work with his followers (Pentecost). Pentecost ends this season by recalling the sending of the Holy Spirit upon his followers, empowering them to proclaim the good news to all people. The Church is commissioned. The vestments for Easter are white, symbolizing "new life"; for Pentecost they are red, symbolizing the strength of the Spirit—"on fire" with life.

Ordinary Time unfolds the mystery of Christ's life in all its fullness by recalling for the community the events of the three years of his public ministry. Ordinary time characterizes the periods between Christmas/Lent and Pentecost/Advent. Green is worn as a sign of the continual life and growth of the Church.

Holy Days are celebrations of key mysteries of the faith of the Christian community. Participation in the eucharistic celebration is required in the United States on six holy days. They are:

Solemnity of Mary, the Mother of God: dating back to the sixth century, this feast (January 1) proclaims Christian faith in the motherhood of Mary and her role in God's plan.

Ascension Thursday: this feast recalls the completion of Christ's earthly mission and his return to the Father in glory. (See Mark 16:19; Luke 24:50; Acts 1:11; 2:34; Romans 8:34; 1 Peter 3:22.)

Assumption of Mary: dating from the seventh century, this feast acknowledges Mary's reception into heaven at the end of her earthly life. Mary's assumption is also a sign of hope to all—a prefigurement of the destiny of all who surrender themselves to God in trust and confidence. This Marian feast is celebrated on August 15.

All Saints: dating from the fourth century this feast (November 1) gathers the community together to honor all those saints who have not been singled out by name or included on the Church calendar during the year.

Immaculate Conception: dating from the eighth century (East) and ninth century (West), this feast professes that Mary was conceived without original sin and was always responsive to God's will. Mary's entire life is the model for the Church and for each Christian. Celebrated on December 8, this celebration provides Christians with the opportunity of deepening their own responsiveness to the presence of God in their lives.

Christmas: this feast, in a sense, is where it all begins. The Eternal One enters human history, and the calendar is rewritten. No longer is the world B.C.; time is now computed A.D. It is a time for new beginnings, new hopes, and new celebrations. Since 354, the Christian community has set aside this day (December

25) to gather together and remember that the "Word was made flesh and dwelled among us."

The entire "liturgical year" or "Church calendar" is linked to the celebration of the Eucharist. "For the Eucharist contains the entire spiritual good of the Church, namely Christ himself, our Passover and living bread, offering through his flesh, living and life-giving in the Spirit, life to those who are invited and led on to offer themselves, their labor, and all created things together with him" (Eucharisticum mysterium, n. 6). In the next section we shall strive for a deeper understanding of the ritual of the Mass.

THE ORDER OF THE MASS

Introduction

Prior to the changes initiated by the Second Vatican Council, the celebration of the Mass was characterized by a uniformity of ritual. In all Catholic churches, whether in San Francisco or New York, Madrid or Hong Kong, the Catholic Mass ritual was the same. A traveler could enter any church and participate in a Mass that was easily recognizable. Conformity was considered a sign of the Church's catholicity, its universality.

Today the Church realizes that the faithful in Uganda, France, Laos, Peru and the United States are people living in different cultures, sharing different experiences, with different ways of expressing and celebrating their relationship with God. For this reason, the Second Vatican Council encouraged local churches to adapt the rituals of the Church so that they are fuller expressions of the celebrating communities.

Not even in the liturgy does the Church wish to impose a rigid uniformity in matters which do not involve the faith or the good of the whole community; rather does she respect and foster the genius and talents of the various races and peoples (Constitution on the Liturgy, n. 37).

The purpose of this guideline is to emphasize a dimension of the Church's universality, namely, the full participation of all Church members in its rituals. Therefore, under the direction of the bishops, local adaptations have been introduced "which, according to circumstances of persons and places, best promote the full, active participation of the faithful and are most to their spiritual advantage" (General Instruction of the Roman Missal).

Persons who experience the Catholic Mass for the first time are often intimidated by its complexity and formality. They are "amazed" that everyone seems to know when to respond, when to stand, sit or kneel. This amazement, however, is easily dispelled when they discover the simplicity and basic uniformity of the Mass structure.

This section is designed to help the reader understand this simplicity and uniformity by presenting the complete order of the ritual of the Mass. Typical prayers, common responses, and sample readings are included. Since many options do exist, we have selected commonly used options to serve as examples. Brief explanations of the parts of the Mass follow. Our understanding of the celebration of the Mass may be furthered if the Mass is viewed as a dialogue between God and his people centering in Jesus Christ. In the "liturgy of the word" God speaks to his people who listen. In the "liturgy of the Eucharist" God's people respond by entering into Christ's response, his sacrifice, by making it their own. This dialogue is preceded by "introductory rites" by which the community prepares itself, and is followed by "concluding rites" by which the people confirm that their lives have been changed and that they must now go forth and live accordingly.

Introductory Rites

Entrance Song
Greeting
Priest: In the name of the Father, and of the Son, and of the Holy Spirit.
People: Amen.
Priest: The grace and peace of God our Father and the Lord Jesus Christ be with you.
People: And also with you.

Penitential Rite
Priest: My brothers and sisters,
to prepare ourselves to celebrate the sacred mysteries,
let us call to mind our sins.
You were sent to heal the contrite:
Lord, have mercy.
People: Lord, have mercy.
Priest: You came to call sinners:
Christ have mercy.
Priest: You plead for us at the right hand of the Father:
Lord, have mercy.

People: Lord, have mercy.

Priest: May almighty God have mercy on us,
forgive us our sins,
and bring us to everlasting life.

People: Amen.

(The "Rite of Blessing and Sprinkling with Holy Water"
may take the place of the penitential rite at the
beginning of Mass. See the prayers of the rite which
are located in this text after the "Opening Prayer.")

Kyrie

Gloria (Glory to God)
Glory to God in the highest,
and peace to his people on earth.
Lord God, heavenly King,
almighty God and Father,
we worship you, we give you thanks,
we praise you for your glory.
Lord Jesus Christ, only Son of the Father,
Lord God, Lamb of God,
you take away the sin of the world:
have mercy on us;
you are seated at the right hand of the Father:
receive our prayer.
For you alone are the Holy One,
you alone are the Lord,
you alone are the Most High,
Jesus Christ,
with the Holy Spirit,
in the glory of God the Father, Amen.

Opening Prayer

Priest: Let us pray. *Pause for silent prayer.*
God our Father,
we are gathered here to share in the supper
which your only Son left to his Church to reveal his
love.
He gave it to us when he was about to die,
and commanded us to celebrate it as the new and
eternal sacrifice.
We pray that in this eucharist
we may find the fullness of love and life.

Grant this through our Lord Jesus Christ, your Son,
who lives and reigns with you and the Holy Spirit,
one God, for ever and ever.
People: Amen.

Liturgy of the Word

First Reading

A reading from the Book of Exodus (12:1–8, 11–14)
     The Lord said to Moses and Aaron in the land of
Egypt, "This month is to be the first of all the others
for you, the first month of your year. Speak to the
whole community of Israel and say, On the tenth day
of this month each man must take an animal from the

flock, one for each family: one animal for each household. If the household is too small to eat the animal, a man must join with his neighbor, the nearest to his house, as the number of persons requires. You must take into account what each can eat in deciding the number for the animal. It must be an animal without blemish, a male one year old; you may take it from either sheep or goats. You must keep it till the fourteenth day of the month when the whole assembly of the community of Israel shall slaughter it between the two evenings. Some of the blood must then be taken and put on the two doorposts and the lintel of the houses where it is eaten. That night, the flesh is to be eaten, roasted over the fire; it must be eaten with unleavened bread and bitter herbs.

"You shall eat it like this: with a girdle round your waist, sandals on your feet, a staff in your hand. You shall eat it hastily: it is a passover in honor of the Lord. That night, I will go through the land of Egypt and strike down all the first-born in the land of Egypt, man and beast alike, and I shall deal out punishment to all the gods of Egypt, I am the Lord! The blood shall serve to mark the houses that you live in. When I see the blood I will pass over you and you shall escape the destroying plague when I strike the land of Egypt. This day is to be a day of remembrance for you, and you must celebrate it as a feast in the Lord's honor. For all generations you are to declare it a day of festival, for ever."

Reader: This is the Word of the Lord.

All: Thanks be to God.

Responsorial
Psalm
(See 1 Cor. 10:16). Our blessing-cup is a communion
with the blood of Christ.

Reader: What return can I make to the Lord
  for all his goodness to me?
I will offer libations to my savior,
  invoking the name of the lord.

All: Our blessing-cup is a communion with the blood
  of Christ.

Reader: The death of the devout
  costs the Lord dear.
Lord, I am your servant,
  your servant, son of a pious mother;
  you undo my fetters.

All: Our blessing-cup is a communion with the blood
  of Christ.

Reader: I will offer you the thanksgiving sacrifice,
  invoking the name of the Lord.
I will pay what I vowed to the Lord;
  may his whole nation be present.

All: Our blessing-cup is a communion with the blood
  of Christ.

Second Reading
A reading from the First Letter of Paul to the
Corinthians (11:23–26)

  For this is what I received from the Lord, and in turn
passed on to you: that on the same night that he was

betrayed, the Lord Jesus took some bread, and thanked God for it and broke it, and he said, "This is my body, which is for you; do this as a memorial of me." In the same way he took the cup after supper, and said, "This cup is the new covenant of my blood. Whenever you drink it, do this as a memorial of me." Until the Lord comes, therefore, every time you eat this bread and drink this cup, you are proclaiming his death.
Reader: This is the Word of the Lord.
All: Thanks be to God.

Gospel Acclamation
All: Alleluia, alleluia, alleluia.
Reader: I give you a new commandment:
love one another as I have loved you.
All: Alleluia, alleluia, alleluia.

Gospel Proclamation
Priest or Deacon: The Lord be with you.
All: And also with you.
Priest or Deacon: A reading from the holy gospel according to John (13:1–15)

It was before the festival of the Passover, and Jesus knew that the hour had come for him to pass from this world to the Father. He had always loved those who were his in the world, but now he showed how perfect his love was.

They were at supper, and the devil had already put it into the mind of Judas Iscariot, son of Simon, to betray him. Jesus knew that the Father had put everything into his hands, and that he had come from God and was returning to God, and he got up from table, removed his outer garment and, taking a towel, wrapped it round his waist; he then poured water into a basin and began to wash the disciples' feet and to wipe them with the towel he was wearing.

He came to Simon Peter, who said to him, "Lord, are you going to wash my feet?" Jesus answered, "At the moment you do not know what I am doing, but later you will understand." "Never!" said Peter. "You shall never wash my feet." Jesus replied, "If I do not wash you, you can have nothing in common with me." "Then, Lord," said Simon Peter, "not only my feet, but my hands and my head as well!" Jesus said, "No one who has taken a bath needs washing; he is clean all over. You too are clean, though not all of you are." He knew who was going to betray him; that was why he said, "though not all of you are."

When he had washed their feet and put on his clothes again he went back to the table. "Do you understand," he said, "what I have done to you? You call me Master and Lord, and rightly; so I am. If I, then, the Lord and Master, have washed your feet, you should wash each other's feet. I have given you an example so that you may copy what I have done to you."

Priest or Deacon: This is the gospel of the Lord.
All: Praise to you, Lord Jesus Christ.

Homily

Profession of Faith (Creed)
We believe in one God,
   the Father, the Almighty,

maker of heaven and earth,
of all that is seen and unseen.
We believe in one Lord, Jesus Christ,
the only Son of God,
eternally begotten of the Father,
God from God, Light from Light,
true God from true God,
begotten, not made, one in Being with the Father.
Through him all things were made.
For us men and for our salvation
he came down from heaven:
by the power of the Holy Spirit
he was born of the Virgin Mary, and became man.
For our sake he was crucified under Pontius Pilate;
he suffered, died, and was buried.
On the third day he rose again
in fulfilment of the Scriptures;
he ascended into heaven
and is seated at the right hand of the Father.
He will come again in glory to judge the living and
the dead,
and his kingdom will have no end.
We believe in the Holy Spirit, the Lord, the giver of
life,
who proceeds from the Father and the Son.
With the Father and the Son he is worshiped and
glorified.
He has spoken through the prophets.
We believe in one holy catholic and apostolic
Church.

We acknowledge one baptism for the forgiveness of
  sins.
We look for the resurrection of the dead,
  and the life of the world to come. Amen.

**General Intercessions
(Prayer of the Faithful)**
Priest: My brothers and sisters, as we have heard
God's word of hope and trust, let us now turn to him
with confidence to pray for all our needs and concerns.
(A series of petitions now follow. Included in these are
petitions for: the Church and Church leaders, social
and civic leaders, the world and significant world
needs (hunger, etc.), the sick and recently deceased,
and the local community and its needs. The people
respond to these petitions with a short acclamation—
for example, "Lord, hear our prayer.")
Priest: We place our trust in you, O Lord, confident
that you will hear us. Strengthen us in our prayer
which we offer through Jesus Christ who is risen Lord
forever and ever.
All: Amen.

Liturgy of the Eucharist

Preparation of the Altar and the Gifts
Procession of Gifts
Priest: Blessed are you, Lord, God of all creation.
Through your goodness we have this bread to offer,
  which earth has given and human hands have made.
  It will become for us the bread of life.

People: Blessed be God forever.

(Commingling of water and wine)
Priest: By the mystery of this water and wine may we come to share in the divinity of Christ, who humbled himself to share in our humanity.

(Blessing for wine)
Priest: Blessed are you, Lord, God of all creation. Through your goodness we have this wine to offer, fruit of the vine and work of human hands. It will become our spiritual drink.
People: Blessed be God forever.

(Washing of hands)
Priest: Lord, wash away my iniquity; cleanse me from my sin.

(Invitation to prayer)
Priest: Pray, brethren, that our sacrifice
may be acceptable to God, the almighty Father.
People: May the Lord accept the sacrifice at your hands
for the praise and glory of his name,
for our good, and the good of all his Church

Prayer Over the Gifts
Priest: Lord God,
may the power of this sacrifice
cleanse the old weakness of our human nature.
Give us a newness of life
and bring us to salvation.
Grant this through Christ our Lord.

People: Amen.

Eucharistic Prayer III
Preface
Priest: The Lord be with you.
People: And also with you.
Priest: Lift up your hearts.
People: We lift them up to the Lord.
Priest: Let us give thanks to the Lord our God.
People: It is right to give him thanks and praise.

(Proclamation)
Priest: Father, all-powerful and ever-living God,
we do well always and everywhere to give you thanks.
When your children sinned
and wandered far from your friendship,
you reunited them with yourself
through the blood of your Son
and the power of the Holy Spirit.
You gather them into your Church
to be one as you, Father, are one
with your Son and the Holy Spirit.
You call them to be your people,
to praise your wisdom in all your works.
You make them the body of Christ
and the dwelling-place of the Holy Spirit.
In our joy we sing to your glory
with all the choirs of angels:

(Acclamation)
All: Holy, holy, holy, Lord, God of power and might,

heaven and earth are full of your glory.
Hosanna in the highest.
Blessed is he who comes in the name of the Lord.
Hosanna in the highest.

Priest: Father, you are holy indeed,
and all creation rightly gives you praise.
All life, all holiness comes from you
through your Son, Jesus Christ our Lord,
by the working of the Holy Spirit.
From age to age you gather a people to yourself,
so that from east to west
a perfect offering may be made
to the glory of your name.

(Epiclesis)
And so, Father, we bring you these gifts.
We ask you to make them holy by the power of your
Spirit,
that they may become the body and blood
of your Son, our Lord Jesus Christ,
at whose command we celebrate this eucharist.

**(Institution Narrative and
elevation of bread and wine)**
On the night he was betrayed,
he took bread and gave you thanks and praise.
He broke the bread, gave it to his disciples, and said:
Take this, all of you, and eat it:
this is my body which will be given up for you.
When supper was ended, he took the cup.
Again he gave you thanks and praise,

gave the cup to his disciples, and said:
Take this, all of you, and drink from it:
this is the cup of my blood,
the blood of the new and everlasting covenant.
It will be shed for you and for all men
so that sins may be forgiven.
Do this in memory of me.

(Memorial acclamation)

Priest: Let us proclaim the mystery of faith:
People: Christ has died,
Christ is risen,
Christ will come again.

(Offering)

Father, calling to mind the death your Son endured for
our salvation,
his glorious resurrection and ascension into heaven,
and ready to greet him when he comes again,
we offer you in thanksgiving this holy and living
sacrifice.
Look with favor on your Church's offering,
and see the Victim whose death has reconciled us to
yourself.
Grant that we, who are nourished by his body and
blood,
may be filled with his Holy Spirit,
and become one body, one spirit in Christ.
May he make us an everlasting gift to you
and enable us to share in the inheritance of your
saints,

with Mary, the virgin Mother of God;
with the apostles, the martyrs,
[Saint N.—*the saint of the day or the patron saint*]
and all your saints,
on whose constant intercession we rely for help.

(Memorial Intercessions)

Lord, may this sacrifice,
which has made our peace with you,
advance the peace and salvation of all the world.
Strengthen in faith and love your pilgrim Church on
earth;
your servant, Pope N., our bishop N.,
and all the bishops,
with the clergy and the entire people your Son has
gained for you.
Father, hear the prayers of the family you have
gathered here before you.
In mercy and love unite all your children wherever
they may be.
Welcome into your kingdom our departed brothers
and sisters,
and all who have left this world in your friendship.
We hope to enjoy for ever the vision of your glory,
through Christ our Lord, from whom all good things
come.

(Doxology)

Through him,
with him,
in him,

in the unity of the Holy Spirit,
all glory and honor is yours,
almighty Father,
forever and ever.

People: Amen.

Communion Rite
Lord's Prayer
Priest: Let us pray with confidence to the Father in the words our Savior gave us:
People: Our Father, who art in heaven, hallowed be thy name; thy kingdom come; thy will be done on earth as it is in heaven. Give us this day our daily bread; and forgive us our trespasses as we forgive those who trespass against us; and lead us not into temptation, but deliver us from evil.

(Embolism)
Priest: Deliver us, Lord, from every evil,
and grant us peace in our day.
In your mercy keep us free from sin
and protect us from all anxiety
as we wait in joyful hope
for the coming of our Savior, Jesus Christ.

Doxology
For the kingdom, the power, and the glory are yours, now and for ever.

Sign of Peace

Lord Jesus Christ, you said to your apostles:
I leave you peace, my peace I give you.
Look not on our sins, but on the faith of your Church,
and grant us the peace and unity of your kingdom
where you live for ever and ever.
Amen.
The peace of the Lord be with you always.

People: And also with you.
Priest: Let us offer each other the sign of peace.

Breaking of the Bread

Lamb of God, you take away the sins of the world:
    have mercy on us.
Lamb of God, you take away the sins of the world:
    have mercy on us.
Lamb of God, you take away the sins of the world:
    grant us peace.
May this mingling of the body and blood of our Lord
Jesus Christ bring eternal life to us who receive it.

(Private Preparation
of the Priest)

Lord Jesus Christ, Son of the living God, by the will of
the Father and the work of the Holy Spirit your death
brought life to the world. By your holy body and blood
free me from all my sins and from every evil. Keep me
faithful to your teaching, and never let me be parted
from you.

Lord Jesus Christ, with faith in your love and mercy
I eat your body and drink your blood. Let it not bring
me condemnation, but health in mind and body.

Communion
Priest: This is the Lamb of God
who takes away the sins of the world.
Happy are those who are called to his supper.
People: Lord, I am not worthy to receive you,
but only say the word and I shall be healed.

(Priest's reception)
May the body of Christ bring me to everlasting life.
May the blood of Christ bring me to everlasting life.

(People's reception)
Priest: The body of Christ.
People: Amen.
Priest: The blood of Christ.
People: Amen.

Communion Song

Period of silence or song of praise

Prayer after Communion
Let us pray.
Pause for silent prayer, if this has not preceded.
Almighty God,
we receive new life
from the supper your Son gave us in this world.
May we find full contentment

in the meal we hope to share
in your eternal kingdom.
We ask this through Christ our Lord.

Concluding Rite

Greeting

Priest: The Lord be with you.
People: And also with you.

Blessing

Priest: May Almighty God bless you,
the Father, and the Son, and the Holy Spirit.
People: Amen.

Dismissal

Priest or Deacon: The Mass is ended, go in peace
(or)
Go in the peace of Christ.
(or)
Go in peace to love and serve the Lord.
People: Thanks be to God.

INTRODUCTORY RITES

"The purpose of these rites is to make the assembled people a unified community and to prepare them properly to listen to God's word and celebrate the Eucharist" (General Instruction of the Roman Missal, n. 24).

Entrance Song

The people stand and sing a song or recite a prescribed antiphon as the priest and ministers enter. This action "introduces them to the mystery of the season or feast" (General Instruction of the Roman Missal, n. 25) and sets the tone and mood of the celebration. (A particular variation of this "rite" is "antiphonal singing" which dates to the fourth century. If this variation is used, a psalm is sung by alternating verses between a cantor and choir or congregation.)

Upon entering the sanctuary or presbyterium, the priest and ministers kiss the altar—a gesture of reverence acknowledging the altar as a symbol of Christ. The priest then leads the people in making the sign of the cross. This signing symbolizes two beliefs central to Christianity: God is one, Father, Son, and Holy Spirit, and we are his people saved in, with and through Christ. Our signing ourselves with the cross proclaims our belonging to Christ and our faith in Christ as the way to share in the life of God and the way to establishing a true human community on earth, the kingdom of God.

One of the earliest references to the sign of the cross is found in the writings of Tertullian (c. 160–220): "At every forward step and movement, at every going in and out, when we put on our clothes and shoes—in all the ordinary actions of everyday life, we trace the sign of the cross."

Mass begins by this invocation of the triune God, praises God in, with, and through Christ and ends as the celebration begins—with a blessing invoked over the people in the name of the Father, the Son, and the Holy Spirit.

Greeting

In any human relationship a greeting is the first attempt to welcome another with graciousness and warmth. The three standard scriptural (2 Corinthians 13:44; Romans 1:7; Philippians 1:1–2) greetings in the ritual express "the presence of the Lord to the assembled community" and, in this greeting by the celebrant and response by the people, "the mystery of the Church that is gathered together" (General Instruction of the Roman Missal, n. 28) and the people's awareness of the reality that they are a community is deepened.

Penitential Rite

The Mass celebrates the love and forgiveness by which Jesus destroyed the power of sin and death and united all people to himself as a perfect gift to his Father. In an act of thanksgiving for love and as an admission of our need for continual conversion, the people join with the priest in the penitential rite in asking God for mercy, forgiveness and healing.

This rite is the community's statement of confidence that God is with them. Fittingly placed at the beginning of the celebration, the penitential rite prepares the community to hear God's word, profess its faith, join in prayers of thanksgiving, and share in communion in the life of God.

The most familiar of the variations in the penitential rite is the Kyrie eleison, or "Lord, have mercy," which is a litany-like petition for God's mercy dating from the fourth-century Antioch-Jerusalem liturgy.

The sprinkling and blessing of the people with holy water may replace the penitential rite. This ritual recalls their initial conversion and baptism and symbolizes new birth, regeneration, cleansing and healing (Genesis 1:1–2, 6–9; Exodus 14–15; 40:12–15; Leviticus 8:7; Ezekiel 36:24–26; Psalm 23:1–2; John 3:5; 2 Corinthians 4:6; Ephesians 5:13–14; 1 Timothy 3:5; Hebrews 10:32). The meaning of the sprinkling with holy water is recalled in the new *Rite of Baptism for Children:*

. . . the door to life and to the kingdom of God . . . the sacrament of that faith by which men and women, enlightened by the Spirit's grace, respond to the Gospel of Christ . . . the sacrament by which men and women are incorporated into the Church, built into a house where God lives in the Spirit, into a holy nation and a royal priesthood . . . a sacramental bond of unity linking all who have been signed by it . . . the cleansing with water by the power of the living word (nn. 3–5).

Gloria

The Gloria is an ancient hymn of praise, full of joy and life, whose theme is the reconciliation of God and humankind in peace and love. The origins of this hymn are uncertain, but it surely dates back to the fourth century. It is probable that the Gloria was first used in the celebration of the Eucharist at the Christmas Midnight Mass, and was originally only sung by bishops. In the fifth century the use of the Gloria was extended to Sunday and feast day Masses. This custom continues today. The Gloria is not said or sung during Advent or Lent. Its absence from the liturgy during these two seasons deepens our preparation and anticipation of the coming of Christ into our lives at Christmas and Easter.

Opening Prayer

The priest speaks the opening prayer for the people. In and through this prayer, the theme, mood and focus of each particular celebration of the Mass is summarized. Everyone stands, and the priest, as the person presiding over this particular community, stretches his arms out in a symbol of the new person who stands upright and freed by the power of Christ's resurrection. He then invites the community to prayer, and after a brief moment of silence, during which the community gathers itself, he officially leads them in prayer.

Introduced into the liturgy in the mid-fifth century, this prayer was originally called "the collect" and served as the conclusion of a litany of prayers in which the celebrant collected and summed up the intentions of the people.

The people's response, "Amen," is a biblical affirmation meaning "So may it be." The word is used in the liturgy as an expression of ratification, assent or acceptance. At this point in the liturgy, it is the people's ratification of all that has been celebrated. It marks the conclusion of the introductory rites and the transition into the liturgy of the word.

LITURGY OF THE WORD

The liturgy of the word celebrates a special presence of God to his people *today.*

When the Scriptures are read in the Church, God himself speaks to his people, and it is Christ, present in his word, who proclaims the Gospel.

The readings should be listened to with respect; they are a principal element of the liturgy. In the biblical readings God's word is addressed to all men of every era and is understandable in itself, but a homily, as a living explanation of the word, increases its effectiveness and is an integral part of the service (General Introduction of the Roman Missal, n. 9).

The assembled people, prepared by the celebration of the introductory rites, now listen to God's word. Their attitude is not simply that of the historian looking for information about past events, but more that of the child eager to listen to a parent so that their values, their life may be more deeply formed.

The Scriptures are revered by Jews and Christians alike as a treasure to be cherished and applied to life. They are not a book of past facts, but the focal point of an event—God entering their life *today*. The Jewish people consider the word of God as food. We read in Ezekiel, "The word of God came to me, and I ate it" (Ezekiel 3:1–3); and in Jeremiah we are told: "God told Jeremiah, 'I have put my words into your mouth,' and he responded, 'When I found your words I devoured them' " (Jeremiah 15:16).

Jesus is the fulfillment of God's word, of God's promises. He is the "Word of God" and the "Bread of Life." Jesus boldly proclaimed that he had come to fulfill the old covenant. And Jesus' followers interpreted his life and ministry as a fulfillment of what God had promised Israel. The early Church, at first by word of mouth and later in written form, has passed on this fulfillment of God's word in Jesus in a special way in the writings of the New Testament. The core of this faith is recorded in the Acts of the Apostles:

Peter proceeded to address them in these words: "I begin to see how true it is that God shows no partiality. Rather, the man of any nation who fears God and acts uprightly is acceptable to him. This is the message he has sent to the sons of Israel, the good news of peace proclaimed through Jesus Christ who is Lord of all. I take it you know what has been reported all over Judea about Jesus of Nazareth, beginning in Galilee with the baptism John preached; of the way God anointed him with the Holy Spirit and power. He went about doing good works and healing all who were in the grip of the devil, and God was with him. We are witnesses to all that he did in the land of the Jews in

Jerusalem. They killed him, finally, hanging him on a tree, only to have God raise him up on the third day and grant that he be seen not by all, but only by such witnesses as had been chosen beforehand by God—by us who ate and drank with him after he rose from the dead. He commissioned us to preach to the people and to bear witness that he is the one set apart by God as judge of the living and the dead. To him all the prophets testify, saying that everyone who believes in him has forgiveness of sins through his name" (Acts 10:34–43).

The aim of the liturgy of the word is to proclaim the word of God and elicit a response of faith from the people, for by responding to the spoken word the people respond to Christ. "He (Christ) is present in his word, since it is he himself who speaks when the Holy Scriptures are read in church" (Constitution on the Sacred Liturgy, n. 7).

The liturgy of the word has always been closely connected with the celebration of the Eucharist. From the earliest days of Christianity, readings were customarily shared with the community gathered for the Eucharist. While the original forms of the readings before the Eucharist are uncertain, the Christian community very early imitated the practices of the synagogue liturgy, namely, two readings, a sermon, and a prayer. Evidence from the second century clearly established this similarity. The choice of readings has undergone many changes over the years. But throughout all these changes a simple guideline seems to prevail, namely, to present as much of the Scriptures as possible to proclaim the truths of faith.

Applying this guideline, the lectionary (book of readings) to be used in the celebration of Mass was revised by the Second Vatican Council. The Sunday readings are now based upon a three-year cycle, with each Synoptic Gospel (Matthew, Mark, and Luke) as its focal point. Each Sunday Gospel reading is then paired thematically with a reading from the Old Testament. A third reading, usually a continuous non-Gospel New Testament writing, completes the customary three Sunday readings. During Advent-Christmas and Lent-Easter, all three readings are unified around one theme.

The readings during the week, however, are arranged differently. These readings are based upon a two-year cycle, and there are only two instead of three readings. These consist of either an Old Testament or non-Gospel New Testament reading and a Gospel reading.

All of this might seem confusing and complex at first. But if we keep in mind the place of Sacred Scripture in the life of the community of the Church and remember that we are in the presence of Christ when Scripture is proclaimed to us, the intricacies and problems with the present cycles fade into the background.

Indeed, God's word is living and effective, sharper than any two-edged sword. It penetrates and divides soul and spirit, joints and marrow; it judges the reflections and thoughts of the heart. Nothing is concealed from him; all lies bare and exposed to the eyes of him to whom we must render an account (Hebrews 4:12–13).

First Reading: Old Testament

From the earliest days, the Church has believed in the continuity between the Old and New Testaments. Both focus on the kingdom of God—the reign of God active in the world which will be realized in all its perfection at the end of time. This and other Old Testament themes, such as creation, salvation, prophecy, law, wisdom, etc., are all recapitulated in the person of Jesus, and help to form the presentation of Jesus, his person, life and ministry, by the New Testament writers. So close is the connection between the Old and New Testaments that Christians cannot fully understand the New Testament presentation of Jesus unless they reflect on the Old (Hebrews 1:1–3). For this reason it is an essential component of the liturgy of the word.

Responsorial Psalm or Gradual

The responsorial psalm or gradual comes after the first reading and provides a peaceful and meditative response to God's word. In the synagogue at the time of Jesus, the Jews followed the readings of Scripture with the singing of psalms. Christians borrowed this practice and continue it to the present day in the form of the responsorial psalm.

Second Reading: New Testament

This reading is often called ''the epistle'' because it sometimes is part of a letter written to the early Christian communities or to individual persons to strengthen their faith, to instruct, to guide, to admonish, or correct errors. The second reading performs a similar function today. While addressed originally to a particular situation in the early Church communities, the message of these writings transcends the centuries to motivate contemporary Christians and to deepen their appreciation of the mystery of Christ.

Alleluia or Gospel Acclamation

"Alleluia" or "praise God" announces or acclaims delight and joy in God's wonderful deeds for his people. The people stand, and make this acclamation in song to proclaim the most wonderful deed of God among humankind, Jesus Christ, visually symbolized by the Gospel book held high by the celebrant or deacon.

The Alleluia became part of the Mass in the fourth century by order of Pope Damasus (368–384). It was originally used only during the Easter liturgy, but Saint Gregory (540–604) permitted its use throughout the Church year except during the Church's penitential seasons. This usage continues today. And when the Alleluia is not used during Advent and Lent it is replaced by a verse which is closely connected in theme with the Gospel reading.

At Easter and Pentecost, there is a special poetic introduction to the Gospel which prepares the community for its proclamation. This poem or song, usually sung by the choir, is called the sequence.

Gospel

The Gospel, the focal point of the liturgy of the word, is a reading from one of the four accounts of Jesus' life, death and resurrection. The use of readings from the Gospels ("the memoirs of the apostles") in the Mass is confirmed by Justin Martyr (d. c. 165) in his *First Apology*. And the significance of the Gospel proclamation in Catholic liturgical tradition is its reservation since the fourth century to those persons sharing in the sacrament of orders, namely, deacons, priests, and bishops.

Because of the Gospel's prominence, its proclamation is often honored on Sundays and feasts by great solemnity. There is a procession in which the Gospel book is preceded by servers carrying candles which symbolize the risen Christ as the Light of the World. Upon arrival at the place of proclamation, the Gospel book is incensed, symbolizing both the community's prayer ascending to God and the mystery of God coming to the community. The sign of the cross is always traced upon the forehead, lips and heart by everyone in the assembly. This signing identifies the readings with the teachings of the Lord Jesus who is the source of our faith as it is heard, spoken and given root in our hearts.

Preceding the proclamation, a prayer is said by the deacon or priest who bows in recognition of the privilege given to him:

Almighty God, cleanse my heart and my lips that I may worthily proclaim your Gospel.

So life-giving is the experience of listening to the Gospel that the deacon or priest concludes by proclaiming "This is the Gospel of the Lord," to which the community responds "Praise to you, Lord Jesus Christ." The minister, as a symbol of reverence, then kisses the Gospel book which is a symbol of the Lord, Jesus himself.

Homily (Sermon)

Central to the Christian tradition is the belief that "faith comes through preaching" (Romans 3:13–15). This belief has its roots in the Jewish faith and in the creative power of the word of God to transform human life. In the Jewish synagogue service the Scriptures were read, followed by instruction. Both Jesus and Paul were invited to speak during one of these services (Luke 4:16ff; Acts 13:15). The earliest Christians were Jewish converts who, accustomed to this practice, very naturally continued it in their own eucharistic gatherings.

While the tradition of preaching in Christianity has had its ups and downs, and the liturgical sermon or homily has had its moments of acclaim as well as discredit, the ministry of preaching is basic to the mission of the Church. Because of this the liturgical movement of the twentieth century has striven to renew the homily's essential importance to the Mass. This importance is clearly summarized in the General Instruction of the Roman Missal: "The homily is strongly recommended as an integral part of the liturgy and as a necessary source of nourishment of the Christian life."

Profession of Faith (Creed)

Creeds are symbols of faith. They are written professions of faith summarizing the faith community's search for an ever-deepening understanding of Jesus and his message. There are three main versions of the Creed which were formulated during the first four centuries, namely, the Apostles' Creed (which was not written by the apostles), the Nicene Creed (325), and the Constantinopolitan Creed (381). It is the latter which is most commonly used in the liturgy today, but the Apostles' Creed is permitted at liturgies in which the greater number of participants are children.

An ancient formula, the original use of the Creed was as a profession of faith for those to be baptized during the Easter Vigil. It was only in the sixth century that the Creed was introduced into the celebration of the Mass. Today, the Creed is recited on Sundays and feasts in the Roman rites, while it is recited at every Mass in the Eastern rite liturgies.

General Intercessions (Prayers of the Faithful)

The Prayers of the Faithful are one of the true restorations in the revised rites for the celebration of Mass. These prayers have had their place throughout the history of the Christian liturgical tradition. They are of Jewish origin, coming to Christianity from the synagogue liturgy. For centuries these prayers ceased being part of the Mass. A remnant of them, however, always remained in the Good Friday Service and, at one point in history, in the Eucharistic Prayer (Canon).

They reflect a simple, direct, personal approach to God. Through them the people petition God for the needs of the Church, society, their own parish, persons in need, the sick and suffering, and those who have died. The General Intercessions coming at the end of the liturgy of the word are a faith-filled statement of trust in all that God has told us and done for us:

If two of you join your voices on earth to pray for anything whatever, it shall be granted to you by my Father in heaven (Matthew 18:19–20).

LITURGY OF THE EUCHARIST

The proclamation of the "word" and the eucharistic actions of the Mass have always been integrally "one." By the end of the first century, the basic structure of the Mass as we know it today was formed—namely the Eucharist preceded by the reading of Scripture passages in the context of prayer. The First Apology of Justin Martyr (already quoted) gives testimony to this fact.

As we enrich our understanding of this next phase of the eucharistic celebration, it is important to keep in mind the relationship between "word" and "action" in Christian theology. Speaking of the revelation of God in the Old Testament, the Second Vatican Council writes: "He (God) so manifested himself through words and deeds as the one true and living God that Israel came to know by experience the ways of God with men" (Constitution on Divine Revelation, n. 14). And in summarizing the purpose of revelation in the plan of

God, the same Council clearly identifies for the community of Christ an important pattern for its life:

This plan of revelation is realized by deeds and words having an inner unity; the deeds wrought by God in the history of salvation manifest and confirm the teaching and realities signified by the words, while the words proclaim the deeds and clarify the mystery contained in them. By this revelation then, the deepest truth about God and the salvation of man is made clear to us in Christ, who is the Mediator and at the same time the fullness of revelation (Constitution on Divine Revelation, n. 2).

The Mass, which is the celebration of Christ and his people on earth, continues this pattern of "word" and "deed" until the end of time. The Mass gathers Christ and his people together in a unique way (in a sacramental way) to unite the words and deeds of the community with those of Christ. Through the Mass, a statement is made, namely, the words and deeds of the community of Christ continue and make present Christ's mission *today* in a uniquely visible manner.

The liturgy of the Eucharist has three basic movements, or rites, namely:

I. Preparation of the Gifts: the community prepares to offer itself together with Christ through the symbolic gifts of bread and wine.
II. Eucharistic Prayer: the community unites with Christ in offering itself to the Father.
III. Communion Rite: the community is united with the Father who accepts the offering of Christ and his people.

Preparation of the Gifts

The Preparation of the Gifts has a twofold purpose: (1) to prepare the bread and wine which will be offered as gift and sacrifice to God, and (2) to prepare the priest and the people for the self-offering of their words and deeds, that is, their very lives.

Originally the preparation rite was very simple. People gathered around the table and placed food upon it in a spirit of gratitude and thanksgiving. With time, however, the simple rite became more embellished. Already by the third century, a procession accompanied the presentation of the gifts. Gifts for the poor and the Church were also eventually included in the offerings. By the Middle Ages, however, as the "communal" dimension of the Mass was less evident, the processions ceased, and the preparation rites became "offertory rites" centering around the prayers of the priest.

The Second Vatican Council has restored the "preparation" dimension of these rites as well as the ancient custom of the procession for presenting the gifts of the community to the priest:

It is desirable for the faithful to present the bread and wine which are accepted by the priest or deacon at a suitable place. These are placed on the altar with the accompanying prayers. The rite of carrying up the gifts continues the spiritual value and meaning of the ancient custom when the people brought bread and wine for the liturgy from their homes (General Instruction of the Roman Missal, n. 49).

The prayer which the priest says in preparing the bread and wine is patterned on an ancient Jewish prayer, the Kiddush, recited at the Passover meal: "Blessed art thou, O Lord our God, King of the Universe, Creator of the fruit of the earth. The earth is the Lord's and the fullness thereof."

Commingling of the Water and Wine

The priest puts a drop of water into the wine as he prays: "By the mystery of this water and wine may we come to share in the divinity of Christ, who humbled himself to share in our humanity."

This simple rite is rich in symbolism. In it are symbolized the mystery of Christ and the Church. In Eastern Christianity this mingling symbolizes the mystery of Christ, the water signifying Christ's humanity, and the wine his divinity. In Western Christianity, the mingling symbolizes the union of Christ (wine) and his Church (water). Fittingly, the prayer which is recited as this gesture is carried out is a remnant of a much longer Christmas prayer dating from about the year 1000.

Washing of Hands

This rite reflects a practical need, namely, the washing of dirty hands. In earlier Christianity, the minister who received the gifts from the people needed to wash his hands before participating in the remainder of the Mass, since the gifts were not limited to bread and wine nor collected in "money baskets." Whatever practical reasons the washing of hands had previously, it is now a symbolic action of preparation. "Lord, wash away my iniquity," the priest says; "cleanse me from my sins."

Invitation to Prayer

After preparing the altar table, and blessing and thanking God for his gifts, the celebrant invites the congregation to pray that the gifts will be acceptable to God. The people respond in prayer that God will be praised and the Church blessed by this celebration of the community.

Prayer Over the Gifts

The Prayer Over the Gifts is said by the priest after the congregation stands. Once called the "Secret Prayer," it was previously recited in a quiet voice—a gesture emphasizing the mystery and sacredness of the actions of the Mass. Now, the Prayer Over the Gifts is said in a loud voice. This small change in the revised rite of the Mass highlights the Church's teaching that the Mass is a public, community action in which all members have a truly participatory function. This prayer concludes the Preparation of the Gifts and serves as a transition to the second movement of the liturgy of the Eucharist, namely, the Eucharistic Prayer.

Eucharistic Prayer

The Eucharistic Prayer is the Church's great thanksgiving prayer praising God the Father for his wonderful deeds among humankind, especially for the expression of his love in Jesus Christ. The word "Eucharist" comes from the Greek *eucharistien,* meaning "to give thanks with praise and favor," and was a translation of the Hebrew *barak* meaning "to bless" in the sense of praising the goodness of God. It was in this sense that the one who presided over the Passover meal "blessed" God. It was in this sense that Jesus "blessed" his Father as he presided over the Last Passover Supper which he shared with his disciples, gave thanks over the bread and wine, and blessed God for his constant love and mercy.

The first Christians followed Jesus' example and employed the patterns of the Jewish "blessings" in their celebrations of the Eucharist. At first these "blessings" or eucharistic prayers were improvised by the celebrant as he recalled the Lord's celebration of the Last Supper. But by the third century, we have documentation that these prayers were being handed on in written form (The Apostolic Tradition of Hippolytus). Today, there are four Eucharistic Prayers commonly used in the Roman Liturgy:

Eucharistic Prayer I

Known as the Roman Canon, this prayer dates to the late fourth century and was in use when the official language of the Church changed from Greek to Latin. Eucharistic Prayer I highlights the purpose of the Mass when from its opening it speaks of giving "praise and thanksgiving (to the Father) through Jesus Christ (his) Son."

Eucharistic Prayer II

This reflects the most ancient eucharistic prayer known, namely, the prayer of Hippolytus. Eucharistic

Prayer II has its own preface which speaks of Jesus "as the Word through whom you (the Father) made the universe, the Savior you sent to redeem us."

Eucharistic Prayer III

This is a mixture of ancient texts used in various liturgies throughout the Eastern and Western Church and will serve as a model in this book.

Eucharistic Prayer IV

Eucharistic Prayer IV is the most fully scripturally based of the eucharistic prayers. It recounts the history of salvation, the significance of Jesus' earthly ministry and his proclamation of good news to the poor and oppressed. This prayer also has a special preface which complements the salvific events enumerated in the Eucharistic Prayer itself.

In addition to the four most commonly used eucharistic prayers, there are five other eucharistic prayers presently approved for use:

Eucharistic Prayers (2)
for Masses of Reconciliation

These prayers emphasize the themes of peace and forgiveness. Each of these prayers also has its special preface which emphasizes the theme of these eucharistic prayers. Eucharistic Prayer I speaks of God's constant call of humankind to a "new and more abundant life" despite our continuous abandoning of God. Eucharistic Prayer II praises God for his constant work of reconciliation in a world of "conflict and division" where his "Spirit is at work, when

understanding puts an end to strife, when hatred is
quenched by mercy, and vengeance gives way to
forgiveness.''

Eucharistic Prayers (3)
for Masses with Children

"The text of eucharistic prayers adapted for children
should help them to participate with greater benefits in
the Masses celebra†ed for adults" (Introduction, n. 1).
The preface written for each of these prayers
introduces the theme of each. Prayer I emphasizes
thanksgiving and God's constant caring for his people;
Prayer II, God's love for us; Prayer III, God's presence
in the world, in people, and especially in Jesus. A
unique feature of the second and third eucharistic
prayers for children is the broadening of the children's
participation through the use of additional
"acclamations" by the children in response to the
prayers of the priest celebrant.

All nine eucharistic prayers now in use have the
same basic components of (a) prayer, (b) blessing, and
(c) thanksgiving. The balance of praise and thanksgiving
blends with the responses of the congregation. The
priest, conscious of being in the presence of
"Someone" who is infinitely good, loving and
generous, prays these prayers with outstretched arms.
A delicate balance and serenity mark all these
magnificent prayers as they summarize the belief and
trust of the Christian community in their Lord, Jesus. In
them the people are united with Christ. They become

a family of worshipers, confident and trusting as they stand face to face with God.

Preface

The word "preface" comes from the Latin *praefatio,* meaning a public announcement. Christians used this word from the eighth century to describe the greeting introducing the prayer of thanksgiving (Eucharistic Prayer). The Preface contains the reasons why the Church has gathered to give thanks. Since these reasons are many, a number of prefaces have been used over the centuries to introduce the Eucharistic Prayer of the Church. The present Preface prayers (91) are in keeping with the liturgical seasons, feast days, and special liturgical celebrations of the Church.

The Preface begins with an introductory dialogue between the priest and people. This dialogue, like other parts of the Mass, has Jewish roots. It reflects Jewish prayers of greeting and invitations to join that were used in giving thanks after meals. The Preface ends in a hymn proclaiming the holiness of God which is adapted from the vision of the prophet Isaiah and Psalm 117.

Epiclesis

As the Preface acclamation "Holy, holy, holy. . ." draws to a close, the priest continues to speak on behalf of the people by praising God for the gift of life and holiness. He then "joins his hands and, holding them outstretched over the offering" of bread and wine, prays an *epiclesis* prayer (from the Greek, meaning "to call down") asking the Father to let his Spirit "come down upon these gifts to make them holy so that they may become for us the body and blood of our Lord Jesus Christ."

This prayer is the first of the epiclesis prayers to be prayed during the Eucharistic Prayer. The second will ask God to unite those who are celebrating the Eucharist.

Institution Narrative

This section is the focal point of the Eucharistic Prayer. Once called the Consecration, it is now referred to as the "institution narrative" and recalls the events of the institution of the Eucharist during the Last Supper meal.

There are four accounts of the Last Supper in the New Testament. Three are contained in the Synoptic Gospels of Mark, Luke and Matthew, and the fourth is in Paul's First Letter to the Corinthians. The four accounts come from two traditions which are seen in the similarities which exist between Matthew and Mark and between Luke and Paul. As these accounts (Mark 14:22–24; Matthew 26:26–28; Luke 22:19–20; 1 Corinthians 11:23–25) are examined, it is easily recognized that the words attributed to Christ in the present-day eucharistic prayers are not found totally in any one of the texts. The words of the institution narrative found in the eucharistic prayers, however, are the result of the tradition of the community bringing the essence of Mark-Matthew, Luke-Paul into a single formula for use in post-apostolic Christianity.

What does it mean to say that the Church "remembers" what Jesus did in these prayers? Remembering has little to do with memorizing certain facts. Remembering is more concerned with evoking, calling forth the presence of another and sharing in that presence. We have a sense of this "remembering" at funerals. People remember stories of the deceased, of things done—humorous incidents, touching moments. Such "rememberings" hold on to the presence of the deceased in a real way. It is not the incidents or moments that are remembered, but the person.

The Jews remember God in a special way each year during Passover. They recall that their ancestors were slaves to the Egyptians, and that God gave them freedom and a new life. They recall that God called Moses to speak for him, and demand of Pharaoh: "Let my people go. . . ." (Exodus 5:1), and that when Pharaoh refused, a series of great tragedies (the plagues) afflicted Egypt. The last of these brought death to the first-born sons of Egypt. During the Passover celebration, Jews recall that they were spared this final death-bearing plague through demonstrating their trust and dependence in God by sprinkling blood from their sacrificial lambs on the doorposts of their houses. The meaning of the event is recalled in Exodus:

When your children ask you, "What does this rite of yours mean?" you shall reply: "This is the Passover sacrifice of the Lord, who passed over the houses of the Israelites in Egypt" (Exodus 12:26–27).

The Israelites then fled into the desert and escaped from the pursuing Egyptian armies as they passed over the Reed or Red Sea into freedom.

In remembering all these events, the Jews remember God. They remember their God who has entered into a covenant with them. They remember their God who promises to be their God, present to them in their own journey through life.

Jews continue to gather each year to celebrate this Passover meal and to remember that with God they can walk through death to life. When they gather, Jews retell the story of the past as prescribed in Exodus 13:8. This retelling is called the *Haggadah.* They also share a meal during this gathering. God is thanked and unleavened bread is broken to remind them that their ancestors ate in haste as they fled to freedom. The bread is blessed and shared; lamb is eaten; wine, shared from one cup, is passed around. Through these rites of remembering, Jews not only recall the events of a past Passover, but they also renew in the present their covenant with God. In this renewal they find the power and strength to walk in freedom as God's chosen people.

Jesus celebrated this Passover meal with his disciples. During the meal, he focused all God's dealings with humankind into the present by identifying himself with the bread and wine, saying, in effect, that he is the new Passover. In him and through his death and resurrection, humanity experiences the passover God intends for all humankind—the crossing from

the slavery of sin to the freedom of love, from the
death of disobedience to the life of grace.

Jesus transformed this ancient festival of national
liberation to one of universal deliverance. Jesus'
transformation of the Passover, however, was not
merely one of words. It was a transformation by
deeds, namely, the deeds of his own death-
resurrection. Jesus became the Paschal Lamb who
offered himself in sacrifice to the Father. His blood
became the new protector of humankind from the
power of death.

Christians remember this new Passover in the
celebration of the Eucharist. By remembering,
Christians enter into and become part of Christ's
sacrifice. In remembering Jesus, crucified and risen,
Jesus becomes really present with the Christian
community, and shares his gift of new life. By sharing
in the sacrificial meal of the Eucharist, Christians
reaffirm the new covenant God has entered into with
humankind, that is, the never-ending love that binds
God to humankind in a relationship which death
cannot destroy.

Elevation of Bread and Wine

There is both a practical and theological reason for
the elevation of the bread and wine after the words of
institution. In the Middle Ages, Christians viewed
themselves as "unworthy" to receive Communion.
This led to the practice of infrequent reception of
Communion—a practice which did not satisfy the

hunger of people for communion with God. The elevation of the consecrated bread and wine helped to satisfy this hunger.

A second reason for the inclusion of the elevation of the consecrated bread and wine is that it is a sign of the Church's belief in the real presence of Christ in the eucharistic bread and wine. This belief was openly denied in the thirteenth century. To counter this denial, Church leaders encouraged the practice of raising the bread and wine so that the people could make an act of faith in Jesus now truly present among them.

Although these situations are not as prevalent today, the Church still continues this centuries-old custom of showing the consecrated host and chalice to the people. Why? This is a moment of faith for Christians! It is a moment of entrusting ourselves to Jesus and committing our lives to the pattern of his Passover. Through the power of the gift of faith, the community and each member of it thrust their lives into the hands of Jesus as he thrusts himself into the hands of the Father. This brief "showing" remembers all there is to remember. Jesus is the way to the Father, and whoever sees Jesus sees the Father.

Acclamation of Faith

The institution narrative draws the community into a proclamation of its faith: "Christ has died, Christ is risen, Christ will come again." This proclamation of belief comes from an ancient Eastern liturgical profession of faith. Such acclamations were common in the more ancient liturgies, but they lost their popularity by the end of the Middle Ages. Appropriately, the reintroduction of this acclamation reinforces the people's participation in the institution narrative. The people are not simple observers, and through this act of faith they are called to enter into the mystery being celebrated.

Anamnesis

We have already spoken much about "remembering." The "anamnesis prayer" focuses the community's remembering on the saving acts of Jesus and evokes from the community a sense of gratitude and thanksgiving. The faithful are also given the opportunity to recall the events of their personal sufferings, deaths and resurrections through which they live daily according to the pattern of the Lord's Passover, and, in remembering, to give thanks for the new life of the Spirit they have often received.

Offering

Saint Augustine wrote, "The Lord left us in this sacrament his body and blood. Now we are called to become his body, and through his mercy we are what we receive." The Church has offered the gifts of bread and wine to God the Father as a sacrifice of Jesus. In this prayer of "offering," the Church now petitions God to accept the offering of the Church so that the eucharistic celebration may achieve the purpose of uniting the members of the Church with each other and with God.

Memorial Intercessions

The Eucharist, celebrated in communion with the whole Church, living and dead, is the offering of all. The priest remembers all Christians living and deceased. He intercedes that all Christians may be strengthened for their journey through life on earth so that their destination, the kingdom of God, may be successfully reached "through Christ our Lord, from whom all good things come."

The reference to Christ, "from whom all good things come," is a vestige of an early liturgical blessing. "All good things" referred to the blessings of the earth, namely, fruit, produce, cheese, olives, bread, which had been brought forward at the presentation of the gifts. These simple gifts expressed the Christian's faith in God as the source of all blessings. They were blessed at this part of the Mass to show the relationship of all earthly blessings to the greatest of God's gifts: himself, in Jesus.

Doxology

The Doxology is a hymn of praise. Various doxologies are included in the New Testament (1 Timothy 1:17; Hebrews 2:7, 9; 1 Peter 1:7; 4:11; Revelation 21:26). The priest lifts up the consecrated host and chalice for all to see and to remember that all things are "lifted up" and made holy in Christ. The community remembers in one great moment of faith that it is "through him (Christ), with him, and in him, in the unity of the Holy Spirit," that all glory and honor is given to the Father. The community responds in a unified act of faith, "Amen." This is our faith. The Eucharistic Prayer comes to a faith-filled conclusion and leads into the Communion rite.

Communion Rite

Communion is an expression of the unity of the body of Christ. To commune is to enter into another's life, to become one with another, to bind oneself with another. Communion is intimacy. Holy Communion is intimacy with God. It is an expression of unity with God, with Jesus, and with all God's people. The Communion Rite helps the community to express its unity, to receive the body and blood of Christ, and to deepen its union with God, with Jesus and with all God's people.

All of the central features of the Communion Rite call attention to this unity. The Lord's Prayer is a prayer of unity; we cannot pray "Our Father" unless we are willing to call others "brother" or "sister." The Sign of Peace symbolizes the breaking down of all divisions and the restoration of harmony. The breaking of the bread symbolizes that we all eat from one loaf, the bread of life. Finally, the community receives Communion by approaching the same table.

Recalling the words of Saint Augustine, we continue our reflections on the Mass: "You are the mystery; you are in the bread. You are in the cup. Become what you have received: the body of Christ."

Lord's Prayer

The Lord's Prayer summarizes the purpose of the life and ministry of Jesus, namely, to share with humankind the special relationship he has with God, a relationship so intimate that humankind can now also address God as "Abba" or Father. The petition for daily bread takes on new meaning in the context of the Mass. Ordinary food satisfies our hunger, but it cannot satisfy the hungers of our heart, our need for intimacy, meaning, and acceptance. Ordinary human relationships very often fail to satisfy these deepest hungers. Only the depth of our relationship with God is food for such hungers. Jesus described himself as the "bread of life" (John 6:48) and promised that those who believe in him would be satisfied: "No one who comes to me shall ever be hungry; no one who believes in me shall ever thirst" (John 6:35).

Forgiveness is at the core of the ministry of Jesus. To be forgiven as we forgive others calls us to match our words with our deeds. Whether the meaning of these words refers to the reality that we are forgiven in the same manner as we forgive others, or that we are forgiven in the act of forgiving others, the meaning is clear: we cannot refuse to forgive others and expect to be forgiven ourselves. By living the call to forgiveness, our unity with God and with others is realized.

Embolism

The last request of the Lord's Prayer is followed by a sequel called the "embolism." This simple, direct prayer flows from a grateful heart. Freed from evil by God's grace, the Christian experiences peace, and is prepared to be a source of peace among others and to foster the kingdom of God on earth. This prayer ends with another brief doxology proclaiming this desire: "For the kingdom, the power and the glory are yours, now and forever."

Sign of Peace

The importance of Christians visibly and concretely being instruments of peace is attested to in Matthew's Gospel: "If you bring your gift to the altar and there recall that your brother has anything against you, leave your gift at the altar, go first to be reconciled with your brother, and then come and offer your gift" (Matthew 5:23–24).

Christians have always greeted each other by offering a sign of Christ's peace. 1 Peter 5:14 states: "Greet one another with the embrace of true love. Peace to all of you who are in Christ." According to the second-century Eucharistic Prayer of Hippolytus, a kiss was given to the newly baptized as a sign of membership in Christ. Justin Martyr asked the people "to greet each other with a kiss" after finishing the prayers. Tertullian called the kiss of peace "the seal of prayer." Pope Innocent I placed this greeting after the Eucharistic Prayer as a sign of the people's assent to it. In the thirteenth century, a crucifix, cross, or some other holy object was passed around to be kissed by everyone in the congregation.

The "Kiss of Peace" was eventually limited to the ministers of the Mass, but the revisions of the liturgy by the Second Vatican Council have restored it to all. The General Instruction of the Roman Missal states: "Before they share in the same bread, the people express their love for one another and beg for peace and unity in the Church and with all mankind" (n. 56). This gesture links love to God and neighbor as an essential response of faith.

Breaking of the Bread

The "breaking of the bread" was the earliest known name for the celebration of the Eucharist (Acts 2:42, 44–46; 7:11; 20:7). For the apostles, the "breaking of the bread" was a sign of the Lord's presence (Luke 24:30).

In Jesus' time it was a custom for the father at the beginning of a meal to take a loaf of bread, offer thanks, give a blessing, and then break the bread into pieces to be passed around to each member of the family. Jesus followed this pattern in the story of the multiplication of the loaves and fishes (Luke 9:16–17).

In our society, we have perhaps lost the significance of sharing. Bread is purchased already sliced, and altar breads are presented as individualized hosts. But to the early Christian, sharing a loaf was a sign of solidarity, of unity, and of family. There was a deep significance in the liturgical action of the "breaking of the bread."

As centuries passed, the rites of the Mass changed. Prepared individual "hosts" replaced larger loaves. Changing cultural and theological movements influenced Church practice. The Second Vatican Council studied the history of these influences upon Church rituals. One of the results of these studies was the renewed importance given to the "fraction rite" or "the breaking of the bread" in the Communion rite of the Mass.

Bread used in Communion is now to look more like actual bread. Some of the bread broken during the "fraction rite" is to be shared with the people. The new instructions also call for a sharing of the one cup on special occasions. This restores the importance of an ancient sign and symbol by which Christians recognize Christ "in the breaking of the bread and in the blessing cup which is the communion of the blood of Christ" (1 Corinthians 10:16–17).

After the priest breaks the bread, he drops a small particle of the bread into the chalice. This ritual of the *commingling of the bread and wine* symbolizes the unity of the body and blood of Christ.

During the breaking of the bread and the commingling of the bread and wine the congregation sings or recites the Lamb of God. This prayer, used in the liturgy since the seventh century, acknowledges Jesus as the new Passover Lamb who is the source of life for the world. It is a clear reference to the blood of the lamb which was sprinkled on the doorposts of Jewish homes to spare their sons from being killed in the Exodus from Egypt (see *Institution Narrative*). The lamb is killed for the Passover meal to commemorate this saving event. John sees Jesus as the new lamb who sheds his blood on the cross. "Look," John the Baptist proclaimed, "there is the Lamb of God who takes away the sins of the world" (John 1:36–37).

During the rite of the breaking of the bread, the celebrant or deacon may put aside a certain amount of the consecrated bread in order to reserve some of it for the homebound and/or sick of the parish. These eucharistic breads are often sent with the priest, deacon or eucharistic ministers to the homebound at the conclusion of the liturgy. This practice emphasizes the reality that the homebound and sick parishioners are truly members of the parish community, and that those who are able to participate in the parish liturgy are deeply concerned about them.

Private Prayers of the Priest

The priest quietly offers a prayer in preparation for his Communion. He asks forgiveness of sins, deliverance from evil, faithfulness to Jesus' teaching, and health of mind and body. As leader of the worshiping community, the priest then first receives the bread and wine. This action invites others to follow his example, "Take and eat. "

Communion

As the body and blood of Christ are held up for the people to witness, the Church proclaims a scriptural acknowledgement of this identity of Christ: "This is the Lamb of God who takes away the sins of the world." The people, acknowledging their deep need for the Lord, respond in faith and confidence with the centurion whose son was helplessly paralyzed: "Lord, I am not worthy to receive you, but only say the word and I shall be healed."

The people process to the altar symbolizing their journey to the kingdom of God. The rich, poor, lame, sick, vigorous, young, old, anxious, doubting, educated, unlettered—all come to the same table where there are no distinctions. Those who commune receive a gift, Christ, and gratefully acknowledge that gift with "Amen." In so doing they affirm that they accept the power of Jesus to transform their lives and to deepen their relationship of love to God and to others.

Saint Augustine says, "If you receive well, you *are* what you have received. Since you are the body of Christ and his members, it is *your* mystery that you receive. You hear the words 'The body of Christ,' and you answer 'Amen.' *Be,* therefore, members of Christ, that your 'Amen' may be true. Be what you see and receive what you are."

The manner of approaching the table (altar) of the Lord expresses the community's faith. We all have memories of being trained for our first reception of the Eucharist and the importance that was placed upon details. Concern is not a new phenomenon. Listen to Cyril of Jerusalem who, as early as 348, spoke of the proper method for receiving the Eucharist:

When you approach (Communion) do not come with your hands outstretched or with your fingers open but make your left hand a throne for the right one, which is to receive the King. With your hand hollowed receive the body of Christ and answer Amen. After having, with every precaution, sanctified your eyes by contact with the holy body, consume it, making sure that not a particle is wasted, for that would be like losing one of your limbs. Tell me, if you were given some gold dust, would you not hold it very carefully for fear of letting any of it fall and losing it? How much more careful, then, you should be not to let fall even a crumb of something more precious than gold or jewels! After receiving the body of Christ, approach the chalice of his blood; do not stretch out your hands, but bow in an attitude of adoration and reverence, and say, 'Amen.' "

Communion is both a very personal and a communal action. Jesus is present to each member of the community as well as to the community as a whole. When we approach the Lord Jesus in Communion, it is faith-in-action. The "Amen" response to the minister's "The body of Christ" is a moment of faith. It has many meanings:

"I believe
  in Jesus as present in the breaking
    of bread
  that this holy bread forms me into a
    temple of the Holy Spirit;
  that the Spirit strengthens me to give
    myself in loving service to others
  just as Christ gave himself to me."

"I remember the Last Supper when Jesus washed the feet of the apostles and linked this action to the Eucharist: 'What I did was to give you an example; as I have done so you must do" (John 13:15).

"When I receive Communion and say 'Amen' to the body and blood of Christ, I say 'yes' to the many ways in which

God speaks to me: in prayer, contemplation of Sacred Scripture, silence, good words, good deeds. I say 'yes' to my responsibilities as a baptized son or daughter of God."

"To break down walls of prejudice, to sow love where there is hatred, peace where there is discord, hope where there is despair, faith where there is doubt, life when what is around me seems to be dying. I say 'Yes' to putting Christ at the center of my life."

Communion is an extravagant gift. It calls for an extravagant response. A passive, rote gesture or a "following of the crowd" is a sign of unawareness of the magnitude of our action. Communion elicits a reflective, lively act of faith. To the proclamation "The body of Christ" we must proclaim "Amen!" In this way our Communion is both a receiving and a giving. Remember: "Be what you see and be what you are." "Though many, one in Christ."

Prayer after Communion

The liturgy of the Eucharist now ends. Our prayers in praise of God and the sacrificial meal are now complete. The people sit in silence to share a moment of personal reflection on the meaning of the mystery just celebrated. Sometimes a musical interlude expresses and deepens this mood. All our actions and words are then drawn together in the Prayer after Communion. The community stands and the priest, with outstretched arms, petitions God to strengthen all present to live the mystery which they have celebrated. The prayer is simple, direct and concise. All that had to be said has been said. We must now prepare to go forth and act. Our words must become our deeds.

CONCLUDING RITES

The concluding rites of the Mass focus upon the sending forth of the community to translate into deeds the words and actions of the liturgical celebration. What has been celebrated must now be revealed in the words and deeds of the members of the assembly as they deal with others and the events of their lives. The celebrant's final instruction brings all the rites of the Mass into focus: "Go in peace to love and serve the Lord."

Blessing. The entire celebration of the Mass has been a blessing—an act of faithful gratitude to God for the gift of himself to humankind in and through Jesus Christ. The people once again sign themselves with the sign of the cross and conclude the celebration as they began, that is, in the name of the Father, and the Son, and the Holy Spirit. What has begun as faith, a gift freely given and freely received, concludes in a crescendo of faith, "Thanks be to God!" Enriched through the words and gestures of worship, the community gladly returns to the hours and days and places of daily living. The Mass now lives in the hearts of Christians. It is no longer simply ritual; the Mass becomes the leaven of humanity.

DEVOTIONAL PRAYERS OUTSIDE OF MASS

Prayers Before Mass
PRAYER TO THE HOLY SPIRIT

Come, Holy Spirit, fill the hearts of your faithful and kindle in them the fire of your love. Send forth your Spirit and they shall be created, and you will renew the face of the earth.

O God, our Father, you teach your family through the light of your Holy Spirit. Grant that by the same Spirit we may be truly wise, and always rejoice in his consolation, through Christ our Lord. Amen.

> Lord God,
> your constant love of man
> has been handed down
> in human words to us.
> In this way you are our God and Father.
> We pray
> that we may eagerly listen

to the words of your Gospel
and in this way be with you heart and soul
in the fellowship of the Holy Spirit.

God,
we break bread for one another
and receive the body,
of Jesus Christ, your Son.
We ask you that,
strengthened by him,
we may live in love and peace
so that he may be present
wherever we speak words
and we may become his body
in this world, for ever.

Your Word Is Near, Huub Oosterhuis

Thanksgiving After Mass

Lord our God,
you have sown in us your word,
given us your Son—
he, who was broken and died for us,
is bread and life
for the world
We ask you
to let us find strength to tread his path,
to let us be for each other

as fertile as seed
and as nourishing as bread
and thus lead a happy life.

We have heard your word, O God,
and have broken bread
for each other.
May this be a sign for us
that you are very near,
that we are your people,
nourished and loved by you.
Never forsake us
and be the light around us
and our firm ground,
and, even more,
be our future, our Father.

Your Word Is Near, Huub Oosterhuis

Various Prayers for Strength and Support

THE HAIL MARY

Hail, Mary, full of grace, the Lord is with thee. Blessed art thou among women, and blessed is the fruit of thy womb, Jesus. Holy Mary, Mother of God, pray for us sinners, now, and at the hour of our death. Amen.

THE SALVE REGINA

Hail, Holy Queen, Mother of mercy.
Hail, our life, our sweetness and our hope!

To you do we cry, poor banished children of Eve!
To you do we send up our sighs, mourning and
   weeping in this vale of tears!
Turn then, most gracious Advocate, your eyes of
   mercy toward us; and after this, our exile, show
   unto us the blessed fruit of your womb, Jesus!
O clement, O loving, O sweet Virgin Mary!

V. Pray for us O holy Mother of God.
R. That we may be made worthy of the promises of
Christ.

Let us pray:
Pour forth, we beseech you, O Lord, your grace into
our hearts, that as we have known the incarnation of
Christ, your Son by the message of an angel, so by his
passion and cross we may be brought to the glory of
his resurrection. Through the same Christ, our Lord.
Amen.

MAY THE LORD SUPPORT US

May the Lord support us
   all the day long
till the shadows lengthen
   and the evening comes,
and the busy world is hushed,
and the fever of life is over,
and our work is done!
Then in his mercy

may he give us a safe lodging,
and a holy rest,
and peace at the last!

Cardinal Newman

PSALM 23

The Lord is my shepherd, I shall not want;
   he makes me lie down in green pastures.
He leads me beside still waters;
   he restores my soul.
He guides me in paths of righteousness
   for his name's sake.

Even though I walk through the valley of the shadow
   of death,
   I fear no evil;
for you are with me;
   your rod and your staff,
   they comfort me.

You prepare a table before me
   in the presence of my enemies;
You anoint my head with oil,
   my cup overflows.
Surely goodness and mercy shall follow me
   all the days of my life;
And I shall dwell in the house of the Lord forever.

EVENING PRAYER

Tend your sick ones, O Lord Christ.
Rest your weary ones,
Bless your dying ones,
Soothe your suffering ones,
Pity your afflicted ones,
Shield your joyous ones,
And all for your love's sake. Amen.

St. Augustine

MY PURPOSE IN LIFE

God created me to do him some definite service. He has committed some work to me which he has not committed to another. I have my mission—I may never know it in this life, but I shall be told it in the next.

I am a link in a chain, a bond of connection between persons. He has not created me for naught. I shall do good. I shall do his work. I shall be an angel of peace, a preacher of truth in my own place while not intending it—if I do but keep his commandments.

Whatever, wherever I am, I can never be thrown away. If I am in sickness, my sickness may serve him; in perplexity, my perplexity may serve him; if I am in sorrow, my sorrow may serve him. He does nothing in vain. He knows what he is about. He may take away my friends, he may throw me among strangers, he may make me feel desolate, make my spirits sink, hide my

future from me—still he knows what he is about.
Therefore I will trust him.

Cardinal Newman

FOR RELIGIOUS VOCATIONS

God, who wilt have all men to be saved and to come
to the knowledge of truth: send forth, we beseech
thee, laborers into thy harvest and grant them to speak
thy word with all confidence, that thy word may be
glorified and that all peoples may know thee, the only
true God, and him whom thou hast sent, Jesus Christ
thy Son, our Lord, who liveth and reigneth with thee,
world without end. Amen.

PRAYER OF ST. FRANCIS

Lord, make me an instrument of your peace!
Where there is hatred, let me sow love;
Where there is injury, pardon;
Where there is doubt, faith;
Where there is despair, hope;
Where there is darkness, light;
Where there is sadness, joy.
O Divine Master,
Grant that I may not so much seek
To be consoled as to console,
To be understood as to understand,
To be loved as to love.

For it is in giving that we receive,
It is in pardoning that we are pardoned,
And it is in dying
That we are born to eternal life.

CHRISTOPHER PRAYER

Father, grant that I may be a bearer of Christ Jesus, your Son. Allow me to warm the often cold, impersonal scene of modern life with your burning love. Strengthen me by your Holy Spirit to carry out my mission of changing the world or some definite part of it for the better. Despite my lamentable failures, bring home to me that my advantages are your blessings to be shared with others.

Make me more energetic in setting right what I find wrong with the world instead of complaining about it. Nourish in me a practical desire to build up rather than tear down, to reconcile instead of polarize, to go out on a limb rather than crave security. Never let me forget that it is far better to light one candle than to curse the darkness, and to join my light, one day, with yours. Amen.

Sample Rite for Communion of the Sick

Jesus' ministry was a ministry of healing, reaching out to those who were sick in body and spirit. The Church continues this ministry of healing in a special way by sharing with its sick members the healing power of the bread of life. The Church appoints ministers (priests, deacons and eucharistic ministers) to bring Communion to those confined to a hospital or their home.

In the following sample of the Rite of Communion of the Sick notice its similarities with the basic structure of the Mass, namely, (a) preparation, (b) listening to the word of God, (c) Communion, (d) prayer, (e) blessing and dismissal. The rite should also be celebrated in a communal manner. Family members and persons caring for the sick Christian are to be invited to participate. Such participation contributes to breaking down the feeling that one suffers in isolation. As a member of the Christian community, the sick person can find support and strength from others in dealing with their illness.

Introductory Rite

The minister approaches the sick person and greets him or her and the others present in a friendly manner. He may use this greeting:
Peace to this house and to all who live in it.
Any other customary form of greeting from Scripture may be used. Then he places the sacrament on the table and all adore it.

Penitential Rite

The minister invites the sick person and those present to recall their sins and to repent of them in these words:

My brothers and sisters,
to prepare ourselves for this celebration,
let us call to mind our sins.
A pause for silent reflection follows.

All say:
I confess to almighty God,
and to you, my brothers and sisters,
that I have sinned through my own fault

They strike their breast:
in my thoughts and in my words,
in what I have done,
and in what I have failed to do;
and I ask blessed Mary, ever Virgin,
all the angels and saints,
and you, my brothers and sisters,
to pray for me to the Lord our God.

The Short Form of the Reading of the Word

A brief passage from Sacred Scripture may then be
read by one of those present or by the minister
himself.

John 6:54–58:
He who feeds on my flesh
and drinks my blood
has life eternal,
and I will raise him up on the last day.
For my flesh is real food
and my blood real drink.

The man who feeds on my flesh
and drinks my blood
remains in me, and I in him.
Just as the Father who has life sent me
and I have life because of the Father,
so that man who feeds on me
will have life because of me.
This is the bread that came down from heaven.
Unlike your ancestors who ate and died nonetheless,
the man who feeds on this bread shall live forever.

The readings for Sundays and feast days could be used here followed by a short summary of the homily and even the general intercessions.

Holy Communion

The minister then introduces the Lord's Prayer in these or similar words:

Now let us pray together to the Father in the words given us by our Lord Jesus Christ.

He continues with the people:

Our Father . . .

Then the minister shows the Holy Eucharist, saying:

This is the Lamb of God
who takes away the sins of the world.
Happy are those who are called to his supper.

The sick person and the other communicants say once:

Lord, I am not worthy to receive you,
but only say the word and I shall be healed.

The minister goes to the sick person and, showing him the sacrament, says:

The body of Christ (or: the blood of Christ).
The sick person answers:
    Amen
and receives Communion.
Others then receive in the usual manner.
After Communion the minister washes the vessel as usual. A period of silence may now be observed.
The minister then says the concluding prayer:
    Let us pray:
    God our Father, almighty and eternal,
    we confidently call upon you,
    that the body (and blood) of Christ
    which our brother (sister) has received
    may bring him (her)
    lasting health in mind and body.
    We ask this through Christ our Lord.
The people answer:
    Amen.

Concluding Rite

Then the minister invokes God's blessing and, crossing himself, says:
    May the almighty and merciful God bless and
    protect us,
    the Father and the Son and the Holy Spirit.
The people answer:
    Amen.
Afterward the minister could visit in a friendly way with the people and leave a copy of the parish bulletin.

DICTIONARY OF THE MASS

Words, Ideas and Symbols Associated with the Mass

ABEL, MELCHISE-DECH Men of the Old Testament (cited in Eucharistic Prayer I) who offered sacrifice to God. Melchisedech offered bread and wine as priest (Genesis 4:4; 14:18; Hebrews 5:6; 11:4).

ADVOCATE One who pleads or speaks for another. Both Jesus and the Holy Spirit are seen as advocates for us, speaking to God on our behalf (John 4:16–26; 16:7; Romans 8:34; 1 John 2:1).

ALPHA AND OMEGA The first and last letters of the Greek alphabet. Their use in Christianity symbolizes Jesus as the origin and fulfillment of creation. ''I am the Alpha and the Omega, the one who is, who was and who is to come, the Almighty!'' (Revelation 1:8).

AMEN A word of Hebrew origin which expresses agreement, affirmation and confidence in the truth of a statement.

ANGELS In Scripture and tradition angels are "messengers" who speak for God. Angels symbolize the inner religious experience of God speaking in a special way (Genesis 16:7; 22:11; 2 Samuel 24:16; Matthew 1:20; 2:13, 19; Mark 1:13; Acts 5:19).

ATONEMENT Atonement is an action by which a person makes up for or repairs an offense or injury. When used in reference to the Mass, atonement refers to the saving effects of Christ's birth, suffering, death and resurrection by which he restores the relationship between humankind and God (at-one-ment).

BRIDE, BRIDE-GROOM The marriage image is used in both the Old and New Testaments to signify God's and Christ's love and fidelity to his people (Hosea 2; Isaiah 54:4ff; Jeremiah 2:2; 3:20; Ezekiel 16:1–43ff; Matthew 9:15; 25:1ff; Mark 2:19 John 2:9; 3:29; 2 Corinthians 11:2; Ephesians 5:25–28; Revelation 18:23).

CHOSEN RACE, These words, once applied to the Israelites in the Old Testament, are given, by

ROYAL PRIESTHOOD, HOLY NATION, PEOPLE SET APART

Peter, to all who believe in Christ (1 Peter 2:9–10).

CIRCUM- CISION

A Jewish ritual signifying belonging to God's people. Since Jesus fulfilled the promises of the old covenant a controversy arose in the early Church over whether or not Gentile (non-Jewish) converts to Christianity should be circumcised (Acts 15:1–12). The early Church decided against universal circumcision. St. Paul said, "Real circumcision is of the heart" (Romans 2:25–29; 4:13; Galatians 5:6; Philippians 3:3; Colossians 2:11).

COVENANT (OLD)

The special relationship that God entered into with Israel in which God promises protection, love and faithfulness, and Israel promised by their love and fidelity to be a special sign of God's presence within the human community (Genesis 6:18; Exodus 19:5, 8, 24).

COVENANT (NEW)

The special relationship God entered into with humankind through Jesus. Jesus announced the new covenant at the Last Supper (Mark 14:24; Luke 22:20; 1 Corinthians 11:25), and ratified it in his own blood.

DOVE
A symbol of the Holy Spirit and of peace (Genesis 8:6–12; Luke 2:2–24; John 1:32).

DIVINE LIFE
The term "divine life" signifies our sharing a special relationship with God. Sacred Scripture speaks of God breathing his own life and spirit in us (Genesis 2:7). Sharing in divine life makes us children of God (Isaiah 43:6; Matthew 5:9, 11; John 1:14, 16–17; Acts 4:33; 17:23; 18:23; Romans 3:24; Galatians 3:26; 4:5–6; Hebrews 2:11).

EAGLE
A symbol of John the evangelist. John's Gospel has often been seen as a testimony to the divinity of Christ. John's "soaring" language earned him the title "eagle." This figure is often sculptured on the pulpit when God's word is proclaimed.

EXILE
Exile refers to estrangement from God, and "sin"—to be turned away from God.

FISH
An early symbol of Christ, coming from the Greek word *ikthus* (fish). The letters I-k-t-h-s stand for the first letters in "*J*esus *C*hrist, *G*od's *S*on, *S*avior." Christians

wore the fish as a secret badge of identity during persecutions. The fish is also a symbol of baptism. As a fish cannot live except in water, the Christian has life through the waters of baptism.

GLORY   God's perfection in love, holiness and goodness. Glory indicates creation's "reflection" of God's holiness, the power and magnificence of God helping his people (Exodus 15:1), and his presence among his people (Luke 2:9, 14).

GOOD NEWS   In general, God's revelation in the Scriptures. Specifically, good news refers to the proclamation that Jesus is Lord. Good news ("Godspel" in Old English) also refers to the Gospel as the joyful message of all that God has done for his people.

GRACE   The relationship of being in favor with God. Our relationship with God is a free and loving gift. Broken by human choice through sin, humankind's relationship with God is restored in Jesus (John 1:17; Ephesians 1:3–7). Jesus is the perfect gift of the Father's saving grace.

IMMORTAL   To be free from the ultimate power of physical death. Immortality refers to the reality that human life on earth is only a stage of human life. Death is a transitional act through which humans pass to share in a life that never ends.

JERUSALEM The place where Yahweh (God) chose for his name to dwell (1 Kings 11:13; 2 Kings 21:4, 23–27). Because Yahweh's presence dwelled in Jerusalem, it was considered a holy city and the center of worship. In the New Testament Jerusalem is associated with the passion, death, resurrection and ascension of Jesus and the coming of the Holy Spirit (Acts 2:1–14). (The "new" Jerusalem signifies the unity of all the faithful, after death, with Christ.)

KINGSHIP, KINGSHIP OF CHRIST A term referring to Christ as Lord of all creation (Ephesians 1:7–10). Jesus proclaimed the kingdom of God's decisive intervention in human history. After the death and resurrection of Jesus, his followers realized that he was the embodiment of God's kingdom. They then began to proclaim Jesus as Lord and King (Matthew 5:43–48; 12:7; 22:34–40; 25:31–46; John 14:21).

LION Symbol of Mark the evangelist. Mark places great emphasis on the royal dignity of Christ and his resurrection. The lion is one of the four animals which appear in the prophecy of Ezekiel.

LORD The title applied to Christ in the New Testament. "God has made both Lord and Messiah this Jesus whom you crucified" (Acts 2:36). Belief in the Lordship of Jesus is at the core of Christian faith and of the apostolic preaching.

MAN Symbol of Matthew the evangelist who emphasized the humanity of Christ.

MEDIATOR The person, Jesus, who establishes and maintains a relationship between God the Father and humankind in a special and final way (1 Timothy 2:5; Hebrews 9:15; 12:24).

MYSTERY The saving life and work of Jesus.

OIL OF GLADNESS Oils, used in worship in Israel and in Christianity, are signs of gladness, healing, joy, and designation of a person for a special service.

OX Symbol of Luke the evangelist. Luke emphasizes the sacrificial aspects of the life and death of Jesus. The ox has also been used as a symbol of Christ.

PASCH, PASCHAL, PASSOVER The redeeming work of Christ—his passion, death and resurrection. Jesus is the paschal Lamb of God, the new Passover. In Jesus and through his sacrifice, we pass over "from sin to forgiveness, from death to life."

PILGRIMAGE   Humankind's journey to God. Pilgrimage indicates a person's response in faith to God's grace which looks toward its fulfillment in heaven.

PRIEST, ALTAR, LAMB OF SACRIFICE   Titles given to Jesus. Jesus is the great high priest (Hebrews 6:20) who offers the one perfect sacrifice to God the Father once and for all (Hebrews 10:12) on the "altar of the cross." Jesus is the Lamb of sacrifice who offered his life to the Father for the forgiveness of sins.

PRIEST, PROPHET, KING   Titles given to Jesus. As Priest he offers himself as the perfect sacrifice to the Father; as Prophet he announces the reconciling power of God in our midst, brought about by his words, his works and his presence; as King he presents himself as the embodiment of God's kingdom (John 18:36).

PROVIDENCE   God's loving care for all creation.

REAL PRESENCE   The belief of the Catholic Church that Christ, crucified and risen, is present, by the power of the Holy Spirit, through the words of the priest, in the bread and wine which we receive at Communion.

REDEMPTION   The saving work of Jesus. "Realize that you were delivered from the futile way of life your fathers handed on to you, not by any diminishable sum of silver and gold, but by Christ's blood beyond all price: The blood of a spotless, unblemished lamb'' (1 Peter 1:18–19).

SACRIFICE The offering of something to God by an authorized person who represents a group of people (worshipers). The word means literally ''to make holy.'' One who offers sacrifice makes it holy by offering it to God as an expression of loving self-surrender. Jesus offered himself as the perfect sacrifice to God the Father on the cross. The Mass ritually remembers this one true sacrifice of Jesus.

SALVATION The invitation of God to share in his life through faith, hope and love. Salvation is life; it literally means ''health.'' We receive salvation as a free gift from God through the birth, life, suffering, death and resurrection of Jesus (Romans 5:1). Both the Old and New Testaments speak of salvation (Isaiah 56:1; Luke 2:30; 19:9; Romans 3:24; 5:12; Ephesians 1:7; 1 Timothy 1:15; Titus 2:11).

SHEEP, SHEPHERD The shepherd and sheep were favorite subjects of early Christian art. Jesus is referred to as the Good Shepherd who seeks the lost sheep (Luke 15:3–7; John 10:1–18). The symbol of a young shepherd carrying a lamb on his shoulders was used in the fourth century to depict Jesus. The Pope and bishops are often called "shepherds" because of their people, the flocks. The bishop's staff (*crozier*) which he carries at some liturgical functions symbolizes his "pastoral" office.

SIN   Any action or word by which a person freely and consciously rejects God's offer of love. To sin is to say "no" to God, and to "miss the mark" or purpose of human life (Genesis 3:23; Mark 1:15; 2 Corinthians 5:2).

TRANSUB-STANTIATION   A philosophical term meaning "essential change." The term is used to refer to the "mystery" of the bread and wine being changed, during the Eucharistic Prayer, into the body and blood of Christ while retaining the appearances of bread and wine.

VERNACULAR The language of the people.

The Church Building, Liturgical Vessels and Materials for the Altar

The Church Building

ALTAR — The central furnishing of the church building. The altar is the common table of the assembly on which sacrifice and thanksgiving are offered and from which nourishment is received.

ALTAR OR COMMUNION RAIL — The altar rail reflects a theology of ritual which clearly separated the laity from the ordained. It served as the place at which the laity knelt for the reception of Communion.

BALDACHINO — A dome or square canopy over an altar.

CATHEDRAL — The church in which the bishop's presiding chair (cathedra) is located, and where the main liturgies of the diocese are usually celebrated.

CONFES-SIONAL — A small enclosure in which a person privately confesses or receives the sacrament of penance (reconciliation). These enclosures are being complemented by reconciliation rooms. These are small rooms where a person meets "face to face" with a priest and celebrates the sacrament of reconciliation.

CRUCIFIX A cross bearing the body of the dead Christ which appeared as an object of veneration in the fifth century. The letters I.N.R.I. are the initials of the Latin words placed on the cross as Jesus died: Jesus Nazarenus Rex Judaeorum (Jesus of Nazareth, King of the Jews).

NAVE The main part of a church, usually separated from the aisle by wings or pillars.

POOR BOX A small receptacle into which persons drop offerings to help the poor.

PRESIDENT'S CHAIR The place from which the priest, as leader of the assembly, leads the congregation in prayer.

PRIE DIEU Small bench on which to kneel. It is pronounced "pree-do" and comes from the French "to pray to God."

PULPIT, LECTERN, OR AMBO A standing desk for proclaiming the word of God and preaching. Its beauty and centrality reflect the dignity of the word. A side lectern may also exist to be used for other important, though subordinate purposes, such as leading the songs or making announcements.

SACRISTY   The room in a church used to store sacred vessels, garments for worship, etc. It is also called the "vestry."

SANCTUARY   The area of a church in which the altar, pulpit, lectern, presidential chair and tabernacle are located.

STAINED GLASS   Windows which refract light, a symbol of the contrasts in our lives: light-darkness; life-death; knowledge-ignorance; faith-doubt. Stained glass windows instructed people during the Middle Ages of the great events in Bible history.

STATIONS OF THE CROSS   Artistic representations usually placed on church walls depicting events in the final hours of Christ's life as he was led to his crucifixion. There are fourteen stations showing a Gospel event or popular story handed down by word of mouth. Forming a mental image of the event and praying before each station is a popular devotion dating back to the thirteenth century.

STATUES   Images, sculptures and paintings of holy men and women. Churches have statues as human models of perfection and personal holiness to be imitated.

TABERNACLE   The receptacle in which the consecrated bread and wine (the Eucharist) is reserved so that Communion may be brought to the sick and homebound. In Jewish worship the tabernacle was a wooden framework, covered with curtains, that was carried through the desert and used as a place of sacrifice and worship (Ex. 26—27).

The Liturgical Vessels and Materials

ASHES A symbol of human frailty and need for conversion (Numbers 19:9; Judith 9:1; Jonah 3:6; Matthew 11:21; Luke 10:13). Catholics put ashes (made from the palms of the previous year's Palm Sunday) on their foreheads on Ash Wednesday to mark the beginning of Lent.

CHALICE The cup used to contain the wine consecrated in the Eucharist.

CHRISM Consecrated oils blessed by the bishop at a special Holy Thursday Mass and used in the celebration of the sacraments.

CIBORIUM A receptacle used to hold bread or hosts for consecration and distribution at Communion.

CORPORAL A square white cloth on the altar on which the chalice and paten are placed. The word comes from "corpus" ("body") on which the body of Christ is placed.

CRUETS Small glass bottles containing the wine and water to be used in the Mass.

FIRE (NEW) The fire lighted and blessed in the opening rites of the Easter Vigil. It symbolizes Christ, the Light of the World, who dispels the darkness of sin and death.

HOLY WATER FONT A container of blessed water located at the church entrance into which worshipers dip their hand upon entering and leaving the church. Worshipers bless themselves with holy water as a reminder of their baptism and their commitment to the Lord.

INCENSE A material producing a fragrant odor when burned. It evokes a sense of the sacred and symbolizes prayer rising to God.

LECTIONARY The book containing the Scripture readings used at Mass or other liturgical worship.

PALL Any cloth that covers some object. In Catholic worship it is a hard cloth that covers the chalice (to prevent dust, flies, etc., from getting into the wine). It is also a large cloth draped over the casket at funerals to recall the person's baptism in which he or she "put on Christ."

PATEN A plate (gold, ceramic, or glass) that holds the bread or hosts to be consecrated.

PURIFICATOR A napkin-like cloth used to clean and dry the chalice and other vessels which have held the consecrated bread and wine.

PYX A small receptacle (resembling a pocket watch) used to carry consecrated bread to the sick. It dates back to about 150 A.D.

SACRA-MENTARY The book of prayers used by the celebrant or president of the assembly.

The Ministers of Worship and Their Vestments

Ministers of Worship

ABBOT The head of certain monastic religious orders, elected by the monks to serve as chief pastor and leader of the monastic community. Abbots have certain special rights accorded to bishops.

BISHOP   A successor of apostolic leadership who holds the highest office in the traditional pattern of Christian ministry, and who is the central religious leader of the Catholic community (Acts 20:28–30; Philippians 1:1; 1 Thessalonians 5:12; 1 Timothy 3:1–7; Titus 1:5–10). Bishops govern Church districts (dioceses), overseeing preaching, the celebration of the liturgy and administration.

CANTOR   A person who sings a psalm or other biblical passage between the readings in religious services. A cantor may also be the leader of song.

CARDINAL   A special advisor to the Pope, a cardinal's chief function is the election of a new Pontiff. Cardinals usually are the bishops of key cities throughout the world. Red, the symbolic color of their office, points to their willingness to remain with the faithful during persecution and to die for the Catholic faith.

CELEBRANT   The principal minister, either a bishop or priest, leading the people at worship. He is also called the president of the assembly.

CHOIR OR SCHOLA   A group of people who sing various parts of the Mass either alone or joined by the congregation.

COMMEN-
TATOR
A person who gives explanations and directions to the people about the various parts of the Mass.

DEACON
A minister ordained to serve the community, especially its sick and poor. The deacon may also proclaim the Gospel, preach, assist the priest at Mass and witness marriages. Some deacons exercise this ministry temporarily before they become priests. Others remain deacons permanently and they may, or may not, be married (Philippians 1:1; 1 Timothy 3:8–13).

EUCHARISTIC
MINISTERS
Persons specially instructed and liturgically commissioned to assist the priest in distributing Communion.

LECTOR
A person who has been trained and commissioned to read the word of God at a liturgical celebration.

POPE
The bishop of Rome, the successor of Saint Peter and the visible leader of the Catholic Church throughout the world. The word "Pope" means "father of fathers." From the earliest days of the Church, the Pope was recognized as the chief authority of the Church and as its symbol of unity throughout the Catholic world.

PRIEST   The English word "priest" derives from the Greek word *presbyteros* (elder). It is an ancient term for the sacred office performed by one who enters into the presence of God, offers sacrifice and speaks to him in the name of the people (Exodus 28; 29:38–42; Ezekiel 44:23). In the sacrament of holy orders, bishops confer on the priest the right to celebrate Mass and the sacraments and to "order" the life of the Church through various ministries throughout the dioceses. Jesus is the perfect priest because he offers the perfect sacrifice (Mark 4:24; Acts 14:23; Hebrews 5:1–4).

SERVER   A person who assists the priest at the altar and in the sanctuary.
(ACOLYTE)

USHERS   Persons who greet those entering a church, lead them to their places and take up the collection.

Mass Vestments

ALB   A long, white tunic-like garment worn by priests and ministers at official liturgical celebrations.

CASSOCK   A close fitting garment, usually black (white in warm climates), worn especially in the Roman Catholic and Episcopal

Churches by clergy and laypersons assisting in worship.

CHASUBLE The colored outer garment, worn over an alb, used at the celebration of Mass.

COPE A richly decorated, long flowing cape worn in processions or in festive celebrations. Catholics associate its use with Benediction.

DALMATIC A garment with long sleeves worn on occasion by a deacon.

MITRE A tall hat shaped like a pointed arch, worn by bishops or abbots. It dates to the thirteenth century as a distinct mark of their office.

PALLIUM An archbishop wears this around his neck during the liturgy as a sign of the unity of all ecclesiastical provinces with the Pope who is the bishop of Rome. It is usually made from white wool and decorated with a cross.

STOLE A long, narrow strip of cloth (like a scarf) worn over the shoulder by bishops, priests and deacons as a symbol of their office of service in the Church.

SURPLICE A knee-length, white linen tunic worn by ministers in the sanctuary who assist the celebrant.

VESTMENTS   Garments worn by ministers at liturgical worship. The use of ceremonial garb grows out of the human need to surround important events with color, pageantry and solemnity. The various colors and designs represent cultural expressions and liturgical seasons and feast days of the year (see liturgical colors).

Liturgical Colors

BLACK   Used occasionally at funerals, depending on local custom. Black symbolizes death.

GREEN   Used on Sundays of the year on which no special feast is celebrated. Green symbolizes the triumph of spring over winter, life over death.

PURPLE, VIOLET   Used in Advent and Lent. Purple and violet symbolize sorrow, penitence, preparation and expectation.

RED   Used on feasts of martyrs, Passion (Palm) Sunday, Good Friday and Pentecost, and for Masses of the Holy Spirit. Red symbolizes the power of love, the shedding of blood, and royalty.

WHITE   Used during the Christmas season, Epiphany, Easter and feasts of virgins and confessors. White symbolizes innocence, birth, rebirth, life, resurrection and holiness.

Liturgical Actions, Rituals and Devotions

ABSOLUTION A prayer in which the priest pronounces forgiveness in the name of Jesus and the Church. It points to God's love reaching out to us with an invitation to a change of heart.

ANOINTING OF THE SICK A sacrament celebrating the presence of Christ to the Christian in moments of critical physical suffering. Previously termed "extreme unction" (last anointing), these rites emphasize healing—the healing of our faith to give us the strength to deal with our situation of suffering. The sacrament does not primarily seek a physical healing of infirmities.

ASPERGES The action by which holy water, as a sign of baptism, is sprinkled over the people during the Easter liturgy and occasionally at the beginning of Mass.

BAPTISM The ritual by which a person is initiated into the community and becomes a member of the body of Christ. The word "baptism" refers to the water used in the sacrament and the ancient rite of going down into the water and emerging cleansed from sin. Through baptism a person enters into the death of Christ and rises with the gift of new life.

BLESSED SACRAMENT The consecrated host reserved in the tabernacle in churches for the purpose of adoration and prayer.

BLESSING An invocation of God's favor. Blessing also refers to a gift of life, or happiness, from God, as well as praise of God.

CANON A Greek word meaning "rule, measurement or model," referring to the Eucharistic Prayer from the Preface to the Doxology, signifying that the "Canon" prayer was the norm or rule for worship.

CHRISTE ELEISON *See* Kyrie eleison

CONCELE- BRATION More than one priest celebrating Mass together or with the bishop, symbolizing the unity of their ministry.

CONFIR- MATION A sacrament celebrating the fullness of our incorporation into the Christian community. Confirmation emphasizes our relationship to the Holy Spirit, and our empowerment to continue the work of Jesus in and through our position in society.

EXORCISM A rite infrequently practiced in the modern Church to expel evil spirits. Scripture passages speak of "evil spirits" at work (Matthew 4:11; Mark 1:23–27; Luke 13:16; John 12:31; 1 Corinthians 12:1ff; 1 Thessalonians 2:18; Hebrews 2:14) which act against a person's desire to respond to God's love.

EXPOSITION The showing of the consecrated host in a display vessel, called a monstrance (from the Latin "to show"). Exposition occurs before Benediction, a service of prayer and song in which the people are blessed with the consecrated bread.

FORTY HOURS DEVOTION A public act of worship lasting approximately forty hours so that the faithful may pray and reflect on the meaning of Jesus revealed in the mystery of the Eucharist. The custom probably comes from the late Middle Ages when prayers were said before the "sepulchre" from Good Friday to Easter morning.

FOLK MASS A Mass where the guitar is the predominant instrument and contemporary "folk" music is sung.

GESTURES Bodily movements and positions determined by culture which signify reverence and respect. Bowed heads, kneeling, standing and arms outstretched communicate non-verbally and have universal meaning in religious worship. Gestures create a spirit of reverence, awe and prayerfulness in the worshiping assembly. "Standing" symbolizes our dignity as sons and daughters of the risen Lord. "Kneeling" expresses our receptiveness and humility. "Bows" are gestures of honor and adoration. Outstretched arms symbolize active attentiveness and openness to God.

GREGORIAN CHANT
A style of liturgical singing used in worship since the sixth century, known for its simplicity, balance and ethereal (heavenly) flow of melodies.

HIGH MASS
A term formerly used to designate a more elaborate celebration of the Mass with incense, processions, and music.

LITURGY OF THE HOURS
An official form of Church prayer including Scripture readings, psalms, prayers, songs, sermons from the Fathers of the Church (leading theologians of the early centuries) and petitions said by the clergy and other designated persons. These prayers are grouped in a book called the "breviary."

KYRIE ELEISON, CHRISTE ELEISON
Greek words meaning "Lord, have mercy, Christ, have mercy." This prayer, found in all liturgies dating as far back as the fifth century, is still a common re-

sponse in the penitential rite of the Mass and in litanies used on special occasions.

LAVABO A Latin term meaning "I will wash." The priest says the "Lavabo" prayer at Mass when he washes his hands to symbolize the purification of his heart and mind as he prepares to offer the Eucharistic Prayer.

LESSON A section of Scripture read during the liturgy of the word communicating to those assembled for worship a "lesson" or pattern for daily living.

LITANY A form of prayer in which fixed responses ("Lord, have mercy, Christ, have mercy," "Lord, hear our prayer") are sung or recited after petitions.

LITURGY The body of prayers, rituals, and symbols
(LITURGICAL) used in public worship. In Greek "liturgy" means "actions of the people" in civic functions. The term now applies to those public ceremonies by which the community offers worship to God.

MASS The most consistent and familiar name for Catholic worship. It is not clear where the word originates. It seems to have some connection with the Latin word "missa" (to be sent or dismissed). In the early Church those people preparing for baptism (catechumens) were sent from the church after the sermon. As they left they received a blessing. At the end of the Mass, those already baptized were also sent from the church and received a blessing. Eventually the "missa" came to be synonomous with the dismissal blessing. People began to draw a relationship between the final blessing and the "great blessing" which was the Eucharistic prayer and the blessing of the bread and wine. Somehow our word "mass" grew out of an idea of being sent with a blessing (missa) and has remained the basic word for the Eucharistic celebration.

MATRIMONY   A sacrament celebrating the fidelity and commitment of husband and wife within the Church community. By celebrating their marriage in a sacramental way, the couple attests to their belief that their life is nourished by Christ and the Church, and that, in turn, their life is a witness to Christ and the mission of the Church.

NOVENA   Nine days of special prayers recited publicly or privately to commemorate a special occasion or to pray for a particular intention. The custom probably has some connection to the nine days spent by Mary and the disciples in prayer between the Ascension and Pentecost (Acts 1:12–24).

NUPTIAL MASS A Mass during which the sacrament of marriage is celebrated.

ORDINATION The sacrament of holy orders confering a public ministry of the Church on bishops, priests or deacons. The "laying on of hands," as the bishop prays to the Holy Spirit, is the central action of ordination (Acts 6:1–6; 13:1–3, 20–28; 1 Timothy 4:14–15; 5:22; 2 Timothy 1:6).

PROCESSION An orderly walk to the place of worship highlighting the belief that the people of God are a "pilgrim people." Processions are used on many occasions and for different purposes. They provide an opportunity to set the tone for a celebration to highlight important Christian symbols (cross, bread and wine, the Scriptures). In the procession the worshiping community is represented (laity, servers, lectors, eucharistic ministers, deacons, bishops, priests).

RECONCIL- IATION The name given to the reformed rite of the sacrament of penance (confession). Reconciliation restores a person's relationship of harmony and unity with God and the Christian community. The Church, through the centuries, has faithfully celebrated this sacrament in varying ways.

RITES A formal set of acts, symbols, signs and gestures constituting a religious observance. These actions create a sense of the sacred and the holy by which persons enter into prayerful communication with God. In the Catholic Church there are Western and Eastern rites. The Western (Roman) rites (Africa, Asia, Western Europe, Oceania, North and South America) tend to be concise and simple, placing less emphasis on God as mystery and giving greater attention to Christ's humanity. The Eastern Rites (those of the churches of the Middle and Near East, Greece, eastern Europe, and parts of Africa) emphasize the mystery of God and use more ornate symbols. Each rite reflects the culture, language, art, music, temperament and religious experience of its people.

ROSARY A form of devotion to Mary which remembers Mary's participation in the ministry of Jesus. This form of prayer combines the repetition of prayers ("Our Father," "Hail Mary," "Glory Be to the Father") and resembles a mantra—an Eastern form of repetitious prayer.

RUBRICS Directions or norms for conducting liturgical ceremonies.

SACRAMENTS Special rituals of the Church in which the Christian community celebrates and communicates God's life to his people, given in and through Jesus. There are seven sacraments: baptism, confirmation, Holy Eucharist, matrimony, holy orders, reconciliation (penance) and anointing of the sick.

SIGN See Symbol and Sign.

SYMBOL AND SIGN An object, person or place that points to a truth which is deeper and more profound than can immediately be grasped or seen. The word "symbol" comes from the Greek "syn" (together) and "ballein" (to throw)—literally, to throw together. Symbols at Mass and in religious worship in general are used to "bring together" certain religious truths into a meaningful whole. The early Christians developed and used symbols to help them communicate spiritual realities. The entire liturgy of the Church is built around the function of words, actions and objects which are signs and symbols of the sacred. Some symbols immediately visible during the Mass are candles, bread, wine, the Bible and the cross. Some signs are genuflections, bows, sign of the cross, and prayer gestures of the priest.

Feasts and Titles of Saints

CONFESSOR One who gives heroic evidence of faith and "confesses" in action a faith in Christ (Francis Xavier, December 3; Francis of Assisi, October 4).

DOCTOR A person who bears witness to the ancient tradition of Christian faith, through scholarship in his or her writings. Since the eighth century the Church has recognized six Doctors of the Church in the West: Ambrose, December 7; Jerome, September 30; Augustine, May 27; Gregory the Great, September 3; Catherine of Siena, April 29, Teresa of Avila, October 15. In the East: Gregory of Nazianzus, January 12; John Chrysostom, September 13.

FATHERS OF Men of Christian antiquity who led holy
THE CHURCH lives and are recognized by the Church for faithfulness in their writings to the teachings of the apostles (Clement, November 23; Ambrose, December 7).

HERMIT A person who lives in seclusion devoting his or her life to prayer and meditation (Romuald, June 19).

MARTYR A "witness" to the Gospel proclaimed by Christ. Martyrs give the ultimate witness to their baptismal commitment by surrendering their physical life in death. This act of trust and faith in God is seen as the fullest witness of a Christian's love of God (Stephen, December 26; Justin, June 1; Agatha, February 5).

PASTOR One whose witness to the community is attested to in his care and leadership. A pastor is one who has been entrusted with the spiritual welfare of persons. "From the way he goest about these duties, may you recognize him as a disciple of Jesus, who came to serve, not to be served" (Ordination Ritual) (Ignatius of Loyola, July 31; Vincent de Paul, September 27).

PROPHETS Persons who speak for God. In the Old Testament, the prophets were sent to call the people to conversion. Prophets did not foretell the future (they were not fortune tellers), although they did foresee future destruction as a consequence of the people's refusal to turn from sin to God. In the New Testament, the prophets were those given the charism to interpret the good news and apply it to daily life (John the Baptist, June 24 and August 29).

RELIGIOUS   One who takes promises or vows to a life of prayer and service in the Church, usually in a community of like-minded persons (Francis of Rome, March 9; Frances Xavier Cabrini, November 13).

VIRGIN   Women who lived in unusual holiness and who practiced sexual abstinence as a radical sign of their love for God and their total availability to others in service to Christ (Agnes, January 21; Maria Goretti, July 6).

BIBLIOGRAPHY

Berube, Francoise Darcy and John Paul, *Sacrament of Peace,* New York/Toronto: Paulist Press, 1974.

Casel, Odo, *The Mystery of Christian Worship,* London: Darton, Longmans and Todd, Ltd., and Westminster, Md.: Newman Press, 1959.

The Catholic Liturgy Book, Baltimore: Helicon Press, 1975.

Dalmais, I. H., *Introduction to the Liturgy,* Baltimore: Helicon Press, 1961.

Diekmann, Godfrey, *Come, Let Us Worship,* Baltimore: Helicon Press, 1961.

Flanagan, Neal, *The Eucharist,* Paramus, N.J.: Paulist Press, 1962 (Doctrinal Pamphlet Series).

Gallagher, Joseph, *To Be a Catholic,* New York: Paulist Press, 1970.

—*What Is Liturgy?* Paramus, N.J.: Paulist Press, 1962 (Doctrinal Pamphlet Series).

Gibbons, Joseph, *Whatever Happened to Friday?* Paramus, N.J.: Paulist Press, 1979.

Guzie, Tad, *Jesus and the Eucharist,* Paramus, N.J.: Paulist Press, 1974.

Hardon, John A., *Modern Catholic Dictionary,* Garden City: Doubleday, 1980.

Heffernan, Virginia M., *Outlines of the Sixteen Documents of Vatican II,* New York: America Press, 1965.

Heiburg, Jeanne, *A Journey to Emmaus,* Paramus, N.J.: Paulist Press, 1978 (Sacramental Spirituality for High School Students, Student Book).

Jungmann, Josef A., *The Early Liturgy,* Notre Dame: University of Notre Dame Press, 1959.

Kilmartin, Edward J., *The Sacrificial Meal of the New Covenant,* Paramus, N.J.: Paulist Press, 1965 (Doctrinal Pamphlet Series).

Lange, Joseph and Anthony Cushing, *Worshipping Community,* Paramus, N.J.: Paulist Press, 1975.

Larsen, Earnest, *Holiness,* Paramus, N.J.: Paulist Press, 1975.

Lechner, Joseph and Ludwig Eisenhofer (edited by H. E. Winstone), *The Liturgy of the Roman Rite,* New York: Herder and Herder, Inc., 1961.

McBrien, Richard E., *Catholicism,* Minneapolis, Winston Press, 1980.

McKenzie, John L., *Dictionary of the Bible,* Milwaukee: Bruce, 1965.

Matthews, Edward, *Celebrating Mass with Children,* Paramus, N.J.: Paulist Press, 1975.

Mossi, John, *Bread Blessed and Broken,* Paramus, N.J.: Paulist Press, 1974.

Mitchel, Leonel, *The Meaning of Ritual,* Paramus, N.J.: Paulist Press, 1977.

Rahner, Karl, *Theological Dictionary,* New York: Herder and Herder, 1965.

Rite of Penance (Study Edition), Copyright 1974, International Committee on English in the Liturgy, Inc., All rights reserved, Washington, D.C.

The Roman Missal, Copyright 1973, International Committee on English in the Liturgy, Inc., All rights reserved, Washington, D.C.

Ryan, John Barry, *The Eucharistic Prayer,* Paramus, N.J.: Paulist Press, 1973.

Ryan, Mary Perkins, *Has the New Liturgy Changed You?* Paramus, N.J.: Paulist Press, 1966.

Shaughnessy, James D., *The Roots of Ritual,* Grand Rapids: William B. Eerdmans Pub. Co., 1973.

Trenchard, John and Christopher Gaffney, *The Mass in Pictures,* Baltimore: Helicon, 1975.

Vagaggini, Cipriano, *The Canon of the Mass and Liturgical Reform,* Staten Island, N.Y.: Alba House, 1967.

Wilhelm, Anthony, *Christ Among Us,* Paramus, N.J.: Paulist Press, 1975.